THE
DOOKY CHASE
COOKBOOK

These Two Generations by Elizabeth Catlett

THE
DOOKY CHASE
COOKBOOK

Leah Chase

PELICAN PUBLISHING COMPANY
GRETNA 2019

First printing, April 1990
Second printing, March 2000
Third printing, September 2004
Fourth printing, September 2009
Fifth printing, January 2013
Sixth printing, January 2016
Seventh printing, March 2018
Eighth printing, March 2019
Ninth printing, June 2019

The word "Pelican" and the depiction of a pelican are
trademarks of Pelican Publishing Company, Inc., and are
registered in the U.S. Patent and Trademark Office.

Library of Congress Cataloging-in-Publication Data

Chase, Leah.
    The Dooky Chase cookbook / by Leah Chase.
        p. cm.
    ISBN 978-0-88289-661-8
      1. Dooky Chase (Restaurant) 2. Cookery, American—Louisiana style. I.
Title.
TX715.2.L68C42 1990
641.59763—dc20   89-48272
                                    CIP

Photographs by Lloyd Dennis
Front of jacket: Snowball Man, *by Winston Falgout*

Printed in the United States of America

Published by Pelican Publishing Company, Inc.
1000 Burmaster Street, Gretna, Louisiana 70053
www.pelicanpub.com

Contents

Street Corner Orator by John T. Scott

Preface

The answer to the perennial question, "How did your restaurant get started?", is an oversimplification along the lines of "necessity is the mother of invention." This was the case with the beginnings of black-owned restaurants in general. They did not come about because an ex-chef simply had a knowledge of food preparation and the desire to own a restaurant. The rent had to be paid, and many black women sold dinners and sandwiches in their neighborhoods to supplement their incomes. Restaurants such as Dooky Chase's began in just this unique fashion. A combination of raw talent in the kitchen coupled with the congeniality of a lottery vendor built a meager po' boy stand into the existing establishment at 2301 Orleans Avenue in New Orleans.

In 1941, after years of selling lottery tickets door-to-door and battling with duodenal ulcers for almost as many years, Edgar ("Dooky") Chase, Sr., thought that it would be ideal if he could open a small sandwich shop and sell the tickets from the same location. This arrangement worked quite well, because people who came by to play their favorite "gig" (combination of chosen lottery numbers) often would buy a soft drink or a beer there. Sometimes they would order a chaurice (type of sausage) on French bread.

They all came, even old ladies, to play the lottery or to pick up the list in the afternoon. If it were "3-5-8," then everyone knew that "Dooky" had won, since that was his favorite gig. Another popular gig was the one known as the "Washwoman Gig," 4-11-44.

With "Dooky," Sr., being so popular with the lottery and his wife, Emily, being such a good cook, before long they were outgrowing the little corner. Five years later the lottery passed from the scene, but the shop was still a popular place to go. It was the only place of its kind for black people at the time.

By then, it was time to expand and the most expedient way was simply to incorporate the living quarters next door. So it came to pass that the living area was reconstructed into a dining room that was decorated with chrome chairs, plastic tablecloths, some wall decor, and mirrors surrounded by neon lighting. The menus were handwritten and placed in a folder that was donated by a brewery—sometimes Regal Beer, Jax Beer, and the like.

To this day, people are amazed at the amount of success the restaurant has had given the fact that Dooky had no formal knowledge of the business. The success can only be attributed to Dooky's popularity and Emily's cooking abilities, along with her genuine concern for people. One of Emily's little-known skills was in the area of money management; it was she who arranged for a loan from a local brewery for the initial expansion. However, the restaurant's general ambience shows Dooky's influence, and that part of his personality which expressed "the good life." After all, in the early thirties, Dooky was one of the few black men in New Orleans, if not the only one, who owned a Model T Ford.

Dooky Chase's was "the" meeting place for everyone of all races and walks of life. After high school proms, Dooky's was the only place parents would allow their daughters to go. For that matter, it was often the only place black youngsters of the day, male or female, were allowed to go.

"Upstairs" at Dooky's, an additional, less-formal dining room, was for a long time the center for some of the most interesting political discussions from the early Civil Rights days to today's city politics.

All things considered, the restaurant has truly been a community restaurant. The Chase family has always been involved in civic activities. It would then be safe to say that it is the community's continuous support and appreciation that has contributed so much to the success of the restaurant.

Through the years, the restaurant's menus have changed and its size has changed along with the decor. It has all been to help satisfy the customer.

I met Dooky Chase, Jr., and married him in 1946. When our children were school age I began to get involved in various aspects of his parents' restaurant and eventually landed in the kitchen. I hope you enjoy the Dooky Chase recipes that have grown out of this restaurant's rich tradition.

Acknowledgments

I would like to thank my children and the rest of my family for all they have done for me and the restaurant. I also thank my niece, Cleo Robinson, and my artist friends, who have been wonderful sources of support.

Harriet Tubman by Elizabeth Catlett

Introduction

My mother hated to cook, but that was understandable. She had eleven kids. She had to cook everyday, three times a day.

People who remember that I never cooked while growing up in Madisonville are shocked to learn that I cook for a living now. Cooking had been the job of my sister under me. She would take care of the kitchen and I would take care of "the house." You had to do your share, though, which meant sometimes cooking too. My grandmother was a midwife and a registered nurse in New Orleans. When my mother would have her babies, everyone had to fend for themselves until she got back home.

I came to New Orleans to go to high school because there was no high school in the country. There was a public school in Covington, but public school was a no-no to my daddy because you might run in to too many non-Catholics! There were all kinds of prejudices in those days—prejudice against religion, prejudice against color. So I went to St. Mary's Academy and stayed with my aunt.

That was when I got my first taste of New Orleans, and later on I was happy to come back to the city to work. I had to beg my daddy to let me work in New Orleans when I was eighteen. The only jobs available then were in the factories, sewing. In those days they had any number of factories for shirts, pants, you name it. That was where black Creoles worked. They dressed all prim and proper and went to work and then changed clothes when they got there. When they finished working, they changed clothes again and came out of the factory all prim and proper. Everyone thought I was going to go to work making pants in the factory. I could sew, but I could not see myself sewing all day every day. If you had a job making pockets, that was all you did. You shot out as many pockets as you could in a day. To me, that was boring.

So my first job in New Orleans was in the Oriental Laundry in the French Quarter. I started at the bottom of the business. The women who worked at that laundry were rough. They knew how to fling those clothes around. My job was to shake things out and get them ready for the person who was going to feed them onto this big machine called a mangle. I did everything in a hurry until one woman pulled me aside and told me to slow down. I thought the more I shook out, the faster I would finish. I worked there for about a week before I got a job at a place called the Colonial Restaurant on Chartres Street.

I had never seen the inside of a restaurant in my life when I got the job at the Colonial Restaurant. There were no restaurants for black people to go to back then. The blacks who had restaurants or little shops, like the Creoles, would not be caught dead in somebody else's restaurant.

Later, the restaurant owner closed the place down and opened the Coffee Pot on Royal Street. At first, all we served there were breakfasts and hamburger lunches. We closed at four. There were three of us running the restaurant for Mrs. Bessie Sauveur. We were sixteen, eighteen, and nineteen years old and did short order cooking. One day we asked Mrs. Sauveur to let us serve one special hot lunch and she said okay if we thought we could do it. Our first hot lunch was Creole weiners and spaghetti. People bought it for 60 cents.

When I worked at the Coffee Pot, I always said I wished I owned it. I wished and wished and wished. One day these three guys came around and told me they would buy the restaurant and I could work in it. I thought to myself, "They can buy it, but I won't work in it." I don't trust people enough to have them do something for me and have that hanging over my head like I owe them.

In 1945 I met Dooky. He was a musician and had his band on the road. I never thought I would marry a musician because I hated musicians. They are always into their own little world. I guess I was in my little world then too. In the country we had outdoorsy things and that was more our life-style. When I compared musicians to people from the country, musicians looked like little timid people to me! But I married him in 1946, three months after we met.

I didn't go to work at Dooky's parents' restaurant when we were first married. My children were coming one right behind the other. Despite how I had felt about sewing jobs when I first moved to New Orleans, I started sewing for people. If someone in the neighborhood needed something sewed, I would do it. I had built a big business on it. I made coats and everything. I even sewed all of the drapes when Dooky Chase's was remodeled. I now love to sew.

When the children got a little bit bigger and they all were in school, that was when I went into the restaurant. Dooky's parents had been running things and my husband thought it was time for a change. I agreed to work for three days a week.

I went in thinking things ought to change. Black men were beginning to have jobs in offices, and were going out for lunch. Before you had only seen the postman. I thought we could do just like I did at the Coffee Pot and begin serving hot meals, but I didn't think I was going to be in the kitchen. I thought I was going to be a hostess or something in the front of the restaurant. I expected to greet people at the door and take them into the dining room and seat them, or maybe even set the tables. In those days tables weren't being set in black restaurants. When you went in they would just hand you a fork and a knife or whatever.

But when I started talking about cooking and nobody in the kitchen knew where I was coming from, I had to get back in the kitchen and start creating dishes. And that was where I stayed.

I came from a different background and thought there was no difference between people other than the color of their skin. That was silly. You have to realize other people have their different beliefs and cultures. Sometimes I had to take a step back and see what would fit to the customers, and then other times I would just put things on them until they got used to it. Most of the customers liked the changes I made. There was talk among the older ones that I was going to ruin everything with my attitude, whatever my attitude was.

My life-style and my husband's family's life-style were nothing alike. My mother-in-law was very good to me, but we clashed on a lot of things because I did things so differently. Her idea of fashions and interior decor was totally unlike mine. There was more dissention about what I was doing with the interior part of the restaurant than what I was doing in the pots. The restaurant had basically enjoyed a captive audience from the beginning, so they didn't care much about the food they served. Changing the decor really became the big issue.

We first made a change in the decor in 1957, right after my father-in-law died. Now that was a battle like you won't believe. My mother-in-law used to say my high mind was going to get me in trouble one day. Well, my "high mind" has never gotten me in trouble yet. I like pretty things, although that doesn't mean I am going to have all of them. My mother-in-law wasn't like that. I don't think she ever saw something that really captivated her.

When I had first worked at the restaurant, the wallpaper was black with pink elephants. The first battle was with the decor on the wall. I wanted mirrors on one wall and another wall with red velour and another with something else. In my own mind's eye I can see now that that wasn't the greatest either, but it went over because my mother-in-law liked red. Then I made all of these gold satin draperies and that went well.

When we got to the chairs, she wanted just a plain little chair. I remembered a beautiful chair I had seen at a restaurant in the French Quarter called the Vieux Carré. My mother-in-law didn't like to spend a lot of money at one time and each chair was twenty-five dollars (the armchairs were thirty-five dollars apiece). In 1957 that was a lot of money. But I won the battle, and when I did she said, "Well, I am going to do the upstairs dining room then." I was tired and couldn't battle anymore so I let her. She painted it pink.

Of course I've learned a lot about cooking over the years, so let me tell you not to worry that you don't have time to cook something good. It doesn't have to take all day, but you have to concentrate. You have to love that pot and love what you are doing. Talk to almost any black Creole person about their food and you will hear all the love in the world as they speak. You get hungry just listening to how they put that food together. They really enjoy doing it. I guess it is like Dooky says, you have to love food and love to eat. I go to sleep thinking about food. I have a stack of cookbooks by my bed. You read things or hear ideas and then your mind starts turning.

When I tell people I am from the country in Madisonville, they immediately seem to think "Southern." They think of collard greens and corn bread. That's not necessarily country; that is Southern. In New Orleans you don't have any true Southern cultures either. Here the food is unique. I don't think you are going to get food anywhere else like in New Orleans. It is a mixture of everything; black, Spanish, and French. Our cooking at Dooky Chase's reflects those traditional influences.

Running a restaurant means more than cooking food, though. It's all about service. I've always been taught that one's rent on earth was paid by services rendered to others. One must share whatever one has to help someone else. Whatever knowledge you have of anything is of no use unless you can spread it around. Your energies are best spent on helping others than on yourself.

When I was a child, not one day could pass in our household without us doing something for someone. With eleven of us children—eight sisters, two brothers, and myself—you would think there was enough to do just within our family. But this was not sufficient in my parents' eyes. We had to run errands for Aunt Lou or get water from the well for Grandma. When Aunt Effie had a new baby, someone had to help with her other little ones. And because Cousin Jeannie's sons were away in the armed forces and she had no daughters, she was alone and one of us needed to stay with her at night. All of this, mind you, was undertaken after we completed our homework and all our daily chores at home.

Does this sound like a hard life of sacrifice and sharing? It isn't half as hard as sharing these recipes with you. Not that they are so important to me. Nothing on this earth is so important to me that I would hesitate sharing with anyone. It's just so hard pulling them from my head and getting them on paper after sixteen hours of work in the kitchen. My brain just takes a long recess.

Working in the restaurant business has now become my way of serving others. In 1942, when I was a waitress, we could count the women who waited tables. Men served in the majority of the good establishments. I loved this job. The people were always fascinating to me. I truly loved restaurant business and still do today.

It is the guest who enjoys the meal and services given that makes me happy. It is truly the best feeling there is to see happy people, and to know that in some way you have contributed to that happiness.

One day, though, I will write a book entitled *Cooking Under Pressure,* which will tell about the hard and ugly side of a restaurant business such as mine! It is sometimes funny, sometimes sad, and many times unbelievable.

A NOTE ON MAGNALITE

My husband says that all people from the country like to do is eat, eat, eat. When I get together with all of my sisters in the country, it is endless food. And we are all big on Magnalite cookware. It looks like a Magnalite factory when we have a family reunion. Magnalite is like a religion to us. I use it at home and in the restaurant. In all of these recipes you will see me say, "Get your Magnalite Dutch oven ... get your Magnalite stockpot ... get your Magnalite chicken fryer." Our Magnalite has to stay shiny, shiny, shiny both inside and out. The pots might be ten years old, but they look brand new. My daughter Emily says that is how you can tell the difference between the "sisters'" pots and the sisters' children. Emily's dish might come in a Magnalite pot, but you are probably going to see the grease building up on the bottom. We recently had a picnic in Lacombe and there was a big table that had to be at least twenty feet long full of Magnalite pots. They came in every shape and size. All of the sisters' pots were shiny. Emily laughed and said it looked like we just walked out of the store with them. The children's were not shiny. I go after my pots with a cleanser like a religion. I never realized how much Magnalite we use in my family until that get-together. There was a little of everything and all in Magnalite pots.

THE
DOOKY CHASE
COOKBOOK

Breads and Breakfast Foods

Untitled by Richard Thomas

My mother always made the bread in our family. But I remember a big treat during my childhood in the depression was store-bought bread. So was a piece of sliced toast. I am always fascinated to see how things I grew up on become the "in" thing. Everybody wants home-made bread now and we always wanted store-bought.

We didn't have very big breakfasts on school days when I was growing up—it was usually just a biscuit and strawberry or blackberry jam. But Sundays were a different story. We had to wait to eat until after church, since it was a rule that you can't have anything before holy communion. That's not true today. So on Sundays, after church, we would come home and have eggs and grits and sometimes even chicken for breakfast.

Everyone in my family enjoyed drinking coffee in the morning, even the children, but not me. I only liked cocoa. But since sugar was scarce then, I learned to like it bitter. I still do.

We didn't have cows for milk and we couldn't afford to buy it either. We had orange juice only sometimes, but we were always healthy. All of us children did get whooping cough though—once it was seven children at once! My mother rubbed us with goose grease or elderberry syrup for that.

A common meal for babies then was sweetened, strained oatmeal. I remember the oatmeal boxes had something that has also become an "in" thing now—depression glass. A dessert dish or something in green or pink was actually packed in some of those boxes as a little surprise.

SWEET POTATO BISCUITS

1 tbsp. butter
1 cup cooked mashed
  sweet potatoes
¼ cup sugar
1 egg (beaten)
2 tbsp. baking powder
3 cups self-rising flour
½ cup shortening
1 cup milk

Melt butter and add to sweet potatoes. Add sugar and egg. Beat mixture until creamy. Set aside.

Mix baking powder with flour and sift. Add shortening and mix well into flour. Add sweet potatoes and milk to make a soft mixture. Work all ingredients together well. Turn mixture onto a well-floured board. Roll dough out to about ½-inch thickness and cut with biscuit cutter. Place on baking sheet.

Bake in 400-degree oven until biscuits are brown, about 15 to 20 minutes. Yield: 6 biscuits.

SWEET POTATO PONE

When I was growing up in Madisonville, the big thing was to spend the day with a relative or friend. Mother and Aunt Esther were very close, and it was always fun when Aunt Esther came to spend the day. She loved desserts, or anything sweet for that matter, and Mother loved to make sweet potato pone.

Well, one time, Mother and Aunt Esther began to grate the potatoes and fire up the wood stove, all set for this sweet potato pone. As I remember it was all done and out of the oven came the pone all nice and golden. And right on Aunt Esther's foot.

Imagine this piping hot goo on your foot! Aunt Esther was screaming with pain; my mother was crying. Now the thing to do in those days was to pat filé powder over the burned area to draw off the heat. So Mother gets the filé jar and sprinkles some on, making a pasty mess all over Aunt Esther's foot.

Two days later infection set in. Aunt Esther seemed to be in serious trouble; Mother cried for fear she would lose the foot. Well, as it goes the foot healed without amputation. But I never remember seeing another sweet potato pone in that house.

4 large sweet potatoes
3 cups sugar
6 eggs (beaten)
1 cup Pet milk
1 cup water
1 tsp. cinnamon
½ tsp. allspice
1 tbsp. vanilla
1 stick butter
Grated nutmeg

Peel and grate sweet potatoes; set aside. Mix butter and sugar together. Slowly add eggs to mixture and mix well. While stirring rapidly add milk and water. Stir until mixture is smooth. Add cinnamon, allspice, vanilla, and grated sweet potatoes. Grease a glass baking dish. Add sweet potato mixture to baking dish and sprinkle top with grated nutmeg. Bake at 300 degrees for 1 hour until pudding is set. Yield: 6 to 8 servings.

WHOLE WHEAT BREAD

2¾ cups warm water
2 pkg. active dry yeast
½ cup brown sugar
   (packed)
1 tbsp. salt
¼ cup shortening
6-7 cups whole wheat flour
Butter or margarine

Measure water into large bowl; sprinkle yeast over water and add sugar. Set aside for 10 minutes until yeast becomes active. After yeast bubbles, stir in salt, shortening, and 3½ cups of the flour. Beat until smooth. Mix in enough of the remaining flour to make dough easy to handle.

Turn dough onto a floured surface and knead for about 10 minutes until the dough is smooth. (The more you knead, the better the texture.) Place the dough in a well-greased bowl, press it down a little, and then turn the dough over so that the greased side is up.

Cover the dough with a towel and let rise in an unheated oven until double in bulk (about 1 hour). Punch the dough down, divide in half, and roll into rectangles one at a time. Roll each up tightly beginning at the short end; seal edges and place seam side down in well-greased loaf pans. Cover and let rise again until double in bulk.

Heat oven to 375 degrees. Bake 40-45 minutes until golden brown. Remove from oven, brush tops with butter or margarine, and let stand on wire rack until cool enough to cut. Yield: 2 loaves.

If you'd like your bread to be a little less crumbly, substitute 2 cups of all-purpose flour for 2 cups of the whole wheat flour.

For WHOLE WHEAT RYE BREAD, substitute 1 cup of rye flour for 1 cup of the whole wheat flour.

You may also substitute ½ cup granulated sugar plus 2 tablespoons (unsulphured) molasses for the ½ cup of brown sugar.

NO-FUSS WHITE BREAD

2½ cups warm water
2 pkg. active dry yeast
2 tbsp. sugar
½ cup nonfat dry milk
1 tbsp. salt
⅓ cup shortening
7-7½ cups all-purpose
   flour
Butter

Set oven to 375 degrees.

Measure water into large bowl. Sprinkle yeast over water; add sugar and stir. Wait 10 minutes until yeast is active. Add dry milk, salt, shortening, and about 3½ cups of the flour. Beat for 4 full minutes at medium speed. Add remaining flour by hand gradually to form a stiff dough. Toss dough onto a floured surface until no longer sticky. Knead until smooth, 1 to 2 minutes.

Divide the dough in half. Form into 2 loaves and place in well-greased loaf pans.

To bake the same day: cover and let rise until double in bulk. Bake at 375 for 35 to 40 minutes. Remove from pans immediately and place on a wire rack. Brush tops with butter and let cool for 10 minutes. (If softer bread is desired, cover the bread with foil for the 10-minute cooling period.)

To refrigerate before baking: shape loaves; place in large plastic bags, leaving enough room for bread to rise. Refrigerate for several hours or overnight. Prick any air bubbles on surface before baking. Yield: 2 loaves.

ITALIAN BREAD STICKS: Using half the recipe, roll dough into a 15" x 8" rectangle. Cut dough into ½" x 4" sticks. Melt ½ cup butter or margarine and combine with 3 tbsp. grated Parmesan cheese and 2 tsp. poppy or celery seeds. Roll the strips of dough in the mixture and place on a well-greased cookie sheet. Bake at 375 for 25-30 minutes. Yield: about 5 dozen.

SOURDOUGH BREAD

STARTER: Measure into a bowl ½ cup lukewarm water and sprinkle 1 package of yeast. Stir until the yeast is dissolved and add 2 cups of lukewarm water, 1 tablespoon sugar, 1 tablespoon salt, and 2 cups sifted all-purpose flour. Mix well. Cover the bowl loosely (with a saucer or plate) and let it stand for 3 or 4 days at room temperature, stirring the mixture down each day.

1 cup sourdough starter
½ cup milk
2 tbsp. sugar
1 tbsp. shortening
3-4 cups sifted all-purpose
**   flour**
More shortening

After the starter is ready, measure into a bowl 1 cup of the starter. Scald the milk and stir in sugar and shortening. Cool the mixture to lukewarm and add the starter. Stir in enough flour to make a stiff dough. Turn the dough onto a floured surface and knead well for 2 minutes.

Place the dough in a greased bowl and brush the top with melted shortening. Cover with a towel and let the dough rise in a warm draft-free place for about 1 hour and 20 minutes until double in bulk. Punch down and shape into a round ball. Let the dough rest for 10 minutes.

Shape the dough into a loaf and place it in a greased loaf pan. Cover and let rise once more until double in bulk. Now it is ready to bake in a 375-degree oven for about 60-70 minutes until top is golden brown. Yield: 1 loaf.

The remaining starter can be kept in the refrigerator and/or can be increased by adding 1 cup lukewarm water, ½ cup flour, and 1 teaspoon sugar. Cover and let stand until the next day. Starter can be added to pancake batter, biscuit dough, etc.

HERBED ROLLS

2 pkg. yeast
½ cup warm water
¼ cup shortening
½ cup sugar
2 tsp. salt
1 can cream of celery soup
1 soup can of water
7-8 cups sifted all-purpose
  flour
2 eggs
1 tsp. celery seeds
1 tsp. caraway seeds

In a large bowl dissolve yeast in ½ cup warm water. Add shortening, sugar, salt, soup, the can of water, and 3 cups of flour. Beat at medium speed for 4 minutes. Add eggs and beat for 1 minute longer. Stir in celery and caraway seeds. Add enough flour to form a soft dough. Turn onto a floured surface and knead until smooth. Place in a greased bowl, turning once to grease evenly the dough surface. Cover with a cloth and let rise in a closed unheated oven until double in bulk. Punch down and mold into desired shape. Place in a greased pan and let rise until double in bulk. Bake at 400 degrees for 20 minutes or until golden brown. Yield: 12 to 18 rolls.

SWEET POTATO ROLLS

¼ cup warm water
1 pkg. dry yeast
1 cup milk
½ cup sugar
1½ tsp. salt
¼ tsp. cinnamon
⅓ cup butter or margarine
2 cups cooked mashed
   sweet potatoes
1 tsp. lemon juice
1 egg (slightly beaten)
5-7 cups sifted all-purpose
   flour
More butter

Put the warm water into a small bowl and dissolve yeast. Set aside. Scald milk; add sugar, salt, cinnamon, and butter. Stir until butter is melted. Pour over potatoes, add lemon juice, and beat until smooth. Cool to lukewarm, then add egg and the dissolved yeast and mix well. Stir in 2 cups of the flour and beat at medium speed for about 3 minutes. Add enough flour to make a fairly stiff dough.

Turn onto a floured surface and knead until satiny. Place in a greased bowl, grease top of dough, cover, and let rise until double in bulk. Punch down and knead once more, then shape into rolls. Place in a greased pan, cover, and let rise until double in bulk. Bake at 400 degrees for 20 minutes. Brush tops with melted butter. Yield: 12 to 18 rolls.

BAKED CHEESE GRITS

4 cups water
1 cup Quick Grits
½ tsp. salt
¼ cup milk
1 egg (beaten)
1 cup grated cheddar
  cheese

In a medium saucepot bring water to a rolling boil. Add grits and salt. Boil until grits are just done, 10 to 15 minutes. Mix milk, egg, and cheese together. Add to grits, stirring mixture well. Stir until cheese is completely melted. Pour mixture into a buttered baking dish. Bake at 375 degrees for 15 minutes. Yield: 6 servings.

FRIED CHEESE GRITS

This recipe was always done with leftover grits. Nothing was ever thrown away. We loved this with fried ham and Creole tomato slices. Syrup on them is great too.

2 cups leftover cheese grits
1 cup milk
1 egg (beaten)
Flour for dredging
Oil for frying

Cut the grits into square cakes. Dip them into a milk and egg batter, then roll in flour. Fry grits in deep fat until golden, 5 to 6 minutes. Yield: 6 servings.

ORANGE PECAN PANCAKES

1 cup flour
1 tbsp. baking powder
¼ tsp. salt
1 cup milk
½ cup fresh orange juice
1 egg (beaten)
1 tbsp. vegetable oil
½ cup chopped pecans

Mix flour, baking powder, and salt together. Slowly add milk and orange juice. Stir well. Add egg and beat into mixture. Mix batter well and add oil. Beat mixture well to remove any lumps. Drop by tablespoon on hot greased grill (using about 2 tablespoons of batter per pancake). When pancakes begin to cook (bubbles will appear), sprinkle pecans over pancakes and turn. Pancakes should brown on both sides. Yield: 12 small pancakes.

BLACKBERRY JELLY

2 qt. blackberries
3½ cups water
1 box Sure-Jel
5 cups sugar

In a stockpot place berries and cover with water. Bring berries to a boil, then simmer for 5 minutes. Allow berries to cool; squeeze through cheesecloth. Mix Sure-Jel with juice from berries. Place on heat and bring mixture to a rolling boil. Allow to cook for 1 minute. Add sugar and boil for 2 minutes. Remove from heat and skim. Pour jelly into jars and seal tightly. Yield: 2 to 3 pints.

PEPPER JELLY

6½ cups sugar
¼ to ½ cup hot peppers
  (chopped fine)
1¼ cups white vinegar
1 cup green pepper
  (chopped fine)
6 oz. Certo

In a medium stockpot place all ingredients except Certo. Bring to a rolling boil. Cook 1 to 2 minutes on very low heat. Remove from heat and stir in Certo. Bring pot back to heat and cook for 5 minutes. Pour jelly into jars and seal. Red or green food coloring can be added to mixture for desired color. Yield: about 2 pints.

FIG BERRY PRESERVE

3 cups figs (mashed)
6 oz. strawberry gelatin
1 box Sure-Jel
2 cups sugar

In a medium stockpot, combine figs, gelatin, and Sure-Jel. On medium heat, cook until mixture boils. Cook for 3 minutes. Add sugar and boil for 2 minutes. Spoon hot mixture into warm jars. Cover jars with hot lids and rings. Yield: 1½ pints.

BREAKFAST SHRIMP

4 tomatoes (very ripe)
Boiling water
1 stick butter
½ cup chopped onions
¼ cup chopped green
  peppers
2 cloves garlic
  (chopped fine)
2 lb. shrimp (peeled and
  deveined)
1 tsp. paprika
½ tsp. salt
¼ tsp. cayenne pepper
2 fresh sweet basil leaves
1 tbsp. chopped parsley

Dip the tomatoes in boiling water; peel and chop. Set aside. Melt butter in saucepot; add onions, green peppers, and garlic. Sauté until onions are clear. Add the tomatoes, shrimp, paprika, salt, cayenne pepper, and basil leaves. Sauté 10 minutes until shrimp are done. Sprinkle parsley on top. Excellent over grits. Yield: 6 servings.

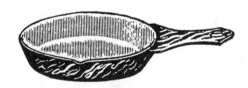

EGGS NEW ORLEANS

1 stick butter
2 tbsp. flour
2 cups Pet milk
1 cup water
½ tsp. salt
⅓ tsp. cayenne pepper
1 tsp. Worcestershire sauce
1 lb. white crab meat
   (thoroughly picked)
6 hard-boiled eggs
1 tbsp. chopped parsley
Paprika and parsley

In a medium saucepan melt butter. Add flour; stir well and cook about 5 minutes. Add the milk, slowly stirring constantly. Add the water, cooking slowly until the mixture thickens. Add the salt, cayenne pepper, Worcestershire sauce, and crab meat. Cook for 5 minutes. Pour into a glass baking dish. Cut the eggs in half and place eggs cut side up onto the crab meat mixture. Sprinkle a little paprika and parsley over the top. Bake in 375-degree oven for 10 minutes. Yield: 12 servings.

Untitled by M. Bengu

People like coming to Dooky Chase's and getting the different soups. They never know what they are going to eat, but they seem to like having to ask what it is. You really have to create those soups. My helpers tease me about my experiments everytime I turn around. They will say, "Don't leave that there too long—Leah will make it into a soup!"

Some of my soups at the restaurant were created when a customer wanted to see a certain food in an unusual recipe. It is just a matter of always working in your mind, figuring what will blend with what.

When I was growing up, Sunday was gumbo day. Sometimes Friday was too. We would have our gumbo or soup at lunch, and if there were any leftovers, my mother added to it for supper. I have collected here some stews, soups, and gumbos. These items are among the most popular with my diners!

GIBLET STEW

½ lb. chicken gizzards
2 cups water
4 chicken wings
2 tbsp. vegetable oil
4 chicken necks (skin
  removed)
2 tbsp. flour
¼ cup vegetable oil
1 medium onion (chopped)
1 large green pepper
  (chopped)
3 cloves garlic (chopped
  fine)
1 tsp. thyme leaves
¼ tsp. cayenne pepper
1 tsp. salt
1 tsp. paprika
Chopped parsley

Properly clean gizzards and cut in half. Place gizzards in water and bring to a boil. Let boil for 10 minutes and reserve the water. Cut chicken wings in half. Discard ends of wings. Heat 2 tablespoons oil in pot. Brown chicken wings and necks in hot oil. Remove chicken parts from pot. Set aside.

Brown flour in ¼ cup hot oil. Add onions and green pepper. Stir well. Drain water from gizzards into the onion mixture.

Add garlic, thyme, cayenne pepper, and salt. Stir well. Add wings, necks, and gizzards to sauce. Add paprika and a little chopped parsley. Bring to a boil, then lower fire and let simmer for 20 minutes. May add a little water if needed while simmering. Yield: 4 servings.

STEWED SNAPPER TURTLE
(Cowan)

This dish so often prepared in every Creole home is an excellent one. Back in the old days, Easter dinner was never complete without cowan.

Turtles were carefully chosen. Females were preferred and were always prodded around the rear legs for eggs. These were cooked right along with the turtle in the spicy gravy.

These turtles are seasonal and are hunted in the spring. I think the art of hunting and catching these turtles is a lost one. As I remember, my Uncle Charlie used a long iron rod. Once into the swampy area, he prodded the mud for the turtles. When he came upon one he used a pole with a hook on the end to retrieve the turtle. He had to do this carefully because they were always snapping at him. Once home, they were stored in a box built underground. Uncle Charlie sold them to family and neighbors—fifty cents for the small ones and a dollar or two for the very large ones. "Small" meant three to four pounds; the large ones could weigh as much as ten to twelve pounds. Now, if you can find one, the selling price is about two dollars per pound on foot—and still worth the price.

Like my mother and all others who enjoy cooking and eating this tasty, spicy dish, I always get the turtle alive. Remove the head and meticulously clean the meat from the shell. If there are any eggs, remove and set aside. I know of no chef willing to take on such a task, but you can believe that this dish is well worth the work. It was always served over rice with a good potato salad on the side and a glass of claret—and that's heaven!

I knew former New Orleans mayor Dutch Morial for a long time, and would always have to cook anything Dutch got dumped on him. Every time his friends would give him something, he would say we had to have a party and I would cook. One year someone had given him about ten or twelve cowan. That meant it was definitely time for a dinner. Here's my recipe for Stewed Snapper Turtle (Cowan).

½ cup vegetable oil
3 lb. turtle meat
Salt and black pepper
⅓ cup all-purpose flour
1 cup chopped onions
¼ cup chopped celery
½ cup chopped green
   pepper
¼ cup chopped green onion
1 tbsp. chopped garlic
1 tbsp. chopped parsley
3 sprigs fresh thyme
1 level tbsp. crushed red
   pepper
1 cup whole tomatoes in
   the juice
1 qt. water
1 level tbsp. salt
1 bay leaf

A well-seasoned cast-iron Dutch oven is the kind of pot for this dish. The next best pot would be a Magnalite Dutch oven.

Pour oil into pot and heat. Season turtle with salt and pepper. Add meat to hot oil, cover, and let simmer for 35 minutes. Remove meat from pot and set aside. Reduce liquid a little and add flour, stirring constantly. Cook flour until brown. Add onions and celery and cook until the onions are soft. Add green pepper, green onions, garlic, parsley, thyme, and red pepper. Stir this mixture well, then add tomatoes and cook for 10 minutes. Add 1 quart of water; stir until mixture is blended.

Add meat to gravy. Add salt and bay leaf. Cook on a slow heat for 45 minutes or until the turtle meat is tender.

If turtle eggs are used, the shells should be pricked all over with a needle before adding them to the gravy. The eggs enhance the flavor of the turtle meat. Add about 2 ounces of dry sherry (not cooking sherry) to gravy. Serve over rice. Yield: 6 servings.

STEWED EGGS

2 tbsp. vegetable oil
1 tbsp. flour
1 medium onion (chopped)
1 8-oz. can tomato sauce
1 pt. water
½ tsp. thyme leaves
1 small green pepper
(chopped)
¼ tsp. cayenne pepper
2 cloves garlic (chopped)
1 tsp. salt
1 tbsp. chopped parsley
1 bay leaf
4 hard-boiled eggs
(cut in half)

Heat oil in saucepot. Add flour and cook for 5 minutes stirring constantly. Add onions and cook until they are soft. Slowly add tomato sauce. Stir well, being careful not to let tomato sauce stick. Add water and continue to stir. Add thyme leaves, green pepper, cayenne pepper, garlic, salt, and parsley. Stir well. Drop bay leaf in mixture. Let simmer for 5 minutes. Add egg halves and simmer for another 10 minutes. Serve over rice. Yield: 4 servings.

CRAWFISH SOUP

4 tbsp. butter
2 tbsp. flour
¼ cup chopped onions
⅓ cup chopped green
   pepper
1 tsp. chopped garlic
3 cups water
1 tbsp. paprika
1 tsp. salt
1 tsp. cayenne pepper
1 bay leaf
1 tbsp. chopped parsley
1 lb. cooked crawfish tails
2 cups half-and-half

In a saucepan, heat the butter on medium heat. Add flour, stirring continuously. Be careful not to brown the flour. Cook for 5 minutes. Add onions and green pepper. Cook until onions are clear. Add garlic. Continue stirring and add water. Simmer about 20 minutes. Add paprika, salt, and cayenne pepper. Add bay leaf and parsley. Add the crawfish and cook for another 10 minutes. Remove from heat. Put mixture into blender and blend until thoroughly mixed. Return mixture to pot. Stir in half-and-half; let simmer for 15 minutes. Yield: 4 servings.

CRAWFISH BISQUE

10 lb. boiled crawfish
1¼ cups vegetable oil
2 cups chopped onions
2 cups chopped celery
1 cup chopped green
    peppers
1 cup chopped green onions
2 tbsp. chopped garlic
1½ tsp. salt
½ tsp. black pepper
1 tsp. paprika
¼ cup chopped parsley
1 cup bread crumbs
Crawfish fat from heads
2 cups plain flour
2 cups whole tomatoes
1 qt. water
3 sprigs fresh thyme
1 whole dried red pepper
½ teaspoon cayenne pepper
1 cup dry sherry
2 bay leaves

Peel and devein crawfish tails. Save heads of crawfish. Chop crawfish meat and set aside. Heat ¼ cup oil in heavy pot. Add 1 cup onion, 1 cup celery, ½ cup chopped bell peppers, ½ cup green onions, and 1 teaspoon garlic. Stir well and cook for 5 minutes. Add crawfish meat, 1 teaspoon salt, black pepper, ½ teaspoon paprika, and 1 tablespoon parsley. Mix well. Make sure onions are soft. Add bread crumbs to mixture. Mix well. Mixture should be tight enough to stuff into heads. Set aside.

Tap heads of crawfish in a bowl to remove fat. Save the fat. Pull legs and eyes from shells. Clean shells well. Stuff mixture tightly into twenty of the heads; discard remaining heads. Roll each stuffed head in flour, coating well.

Heat 1 cup oil in Magnalite Dutch oven. Place stuffed heads in hot oil and cook to a light brown on all sides. Set fried heads aside.

Sift flour that was used to roll heads. Add 1 cup sifted flour to hot oil. Brown flour and add remaining onions; cook until onions are soft. Add remaining celery, bell peppers, green onions, and garlic and stir well. Add whole tomatoes and chop them into mixture. Slowly add water and stir well. Add remaining salt, paprika, and parsley, and add the thyme, dried red pepper, and cayenne pepper. Stir well. Mix the reserved fat in gravy and let simmer on medium heat for 20 minutes. Add wine, bay leaves, and stuffed heads; continue to simmer for 20 minutes. Serve over rice. Yield: 4 servings.

B.L.T. SOUP

Strange, you say! Well, *c'est la vie!* At Dooky Chase Restaurant, iceberg lettuce is bought by the crate. There are so many good green outer leaves that are not very good in salads, but it seems like such a waste not to use them. So we started using these leaves as side dishes, braised in butter.

Another dish was Lettuce Soup. It was this Lettuce Soup that evolved into the "B.L.T. Soup." Having to put a soup on the Lunch Buffet five days a week can really exhaust your list of soups. Therefore, instead of using butter in which to cook the flour, bacon drippings were used for added flavor. Then we decided to crumble the bacon into the Lettuce Soup; and then, for a little color, a few pieces of fresh tomatoes were added and *voilà!—"Potage de Lettuce"* became *"Potage de B.L.T."*

½ medium head iceberg
  lettuce
2 qt. water
1½ tsp. salt
½ lb. bacon
3 heaping tbsp. all-purpose
  flour
¼ cup chopped green
  onions
½ tsp. crushed red pepper
1 tsp. paprika
1 large ripe tomato (cut
  into eighths)

Place lettuce in pot with water and 1 teaspoon of the salt. Remove lettuce and let drain. Reserve the water in which lettuce was cooked. Chop lettuce and set aside. Cook bacon in a skillet until crisp. Remove bacon from skillet and set aside.

Add flour to bacon drippings. Cook for about 6 minutes. Add green onions; stir and let cook for about 4 minutes. Pour this mixture into the water reserved from cooking the lettuce. Add a little of the water to skillet to deglaze. Bring to a boil and add to pot of reserved water. Let liquid come to a boil. Lower heat, then add remaining salt, crushed red pepper, and paprika. Add the chopped lettuce and let cook for 10 minutes. Add tomatoes and cook for about 4 minutes (tomatoes should retain some firmness—don't allow them to become too soft). Break bacon into very small pieces and sprinkle into the soup. Yield: 6 servings.

OLD-FASHIONED OYSTER SOUP

½ cup vegetable oil
2 tbsp. flour
1 large onion (chopped)
¼ cup chopped celery
2 qt. water
6 green onions (chopped)
2 cloves garlic (chopped
   fine)
¼ tsp. thyme
1 tbsp. salt
¼ tsp. crushed pepper
1 tsp. white pepper
36 oysters in their liquid
6 oz. vermicelli
2 tbsp. chopped parsley

Heat oil in pot. Add flour, stirring constantly for 5 to 6 minutes. Lower heat and add onion. Sauté until onions are clear. Add celery and continue cooking for about 5 minutes. Slowly add water and let simmer for 10 minutes. Add green onions, garlic, thyme, salt, crushed pepper, and white pepper. Take out 12 oysters, chop, and add to pot. Add vermicelli and parsley and cook for 10 minutes. Add remaining oysters and liquid. Cook until oysters curl (about 15 minutes). Yield: 4-6 servings.

CHICKEN AND SHRIMP SOUP

One 3-lb. spring chicken
(fryer)
3 qt. water
1 cup chopped onions
1½ cups chopped celery
2 medium carrots
(chopped)
1 lb. shrimp with heads on
1 cup butter
½ cup flour
1 tsp. salt
1 tsp. cayenne pepper
½ tsp. ground thyme

Put chicken in pot with water, onions, celery, and carrots. Boil until chicken is tender. Remove chicken from pot and reserve the liquid. Remove skin from chicken and take out all bones. Cut chicken into small pieces and set aside. Peel shrimp, reserving the heads and shells. Devein and wash shrimp, then set aside.

In a 1½-quart saucepan, melt butter. Add shrimp heads and shells to butter. Sauté for 5 minutes until shrimp heads and shells are bright pink in color. Strain butter into 5-quart pot. Add flour and cook for 5 minutes, but not until brown. Add reserved liquid, salt, cayenne pepper, and thyme. Let cook over medium heat for 15 minutes. Add chicken and shrimp. Cook for about 10 minutes until shrimp are done. Yield: 6-8 servings.

CRAB SOUP

3 medium blue crabs
½ cup vegetable oil
3 tbsp. all-purpose flour
¾ cup chopped onions
¼ cup chopped celery
½ cup chopped green
pepper
1½ qt. water
1 clove garlic (chopped)
1 tsp. whole thyme
½ tsp. cayenne pepper
1 tsp. paprika
1 tbsp. chopped parsley
2 tsp. salt
½ lb. white crab meat

Clean crabs and cut in halves. Heat oil in pot. Add crabs; fry in hot oil for 10 minutes. Lower heat. Remove crabs. Set aside. To the oil, add the flour, stirring constantly. Cook until light brown. Add onions and celery and cook until the onions are translucent. Add the green pepper and cook for about 3 to 4 minutes. Add water, pouring slowly while stirring. Add garlic, thyme, cayenne pepper, paprika, parsley, and salt. Return crabs to liquid; let cook for 30 to 40 minutes. Stir in white crab meat and simmer for 5 minutes. Yield: 6 servings.

NOTE: Female crabs are very good for this recipe.

VEGETABLE SOUP

Daddy would like to see me do different things with the vegetables he grew. One of the things that I finally got him to eat once was vegetables marinated in Italian spices. If I would make a soup with all of the different vegetables and whatnot, he would think I was strange. But when he would taste it, he would appreciate that a soup like that could be made with his vegetables.

This vegetable soup recipe is my mother's, and it always turned into two courses. Once the soup was done, my mother removed the meat and potatoes from the soup as well as any meat from the soup bone. It was also important to take the marrow out of the soup bone. Then she would place the diced soup meat, potatoes, and bone marrow in a bowl, and season it with black pepper, vinegar, and oil to taste. *Ah, mon chéri! Très bon!*

2 lb. beef brisket
1 soup bone (beef with marrow)
4 qt. water
2 cups tomato puree
½ cup chopped onions
2 carrots (cleaned and sliced)
1 medium turnip (cubed)
1 cup shredded cabbage
½ cup cut green beans
½ cup whole kernel corn
1 large white potato (cubed)
2 cups celery (chopped)
½ cup baby lima beans
½ cup green peas
1 tbsp. salt
1 tsp. crushed red pepper
5 oz. vermicelli

In a large stockpot, place brisket and soup bone. Add water and bring to a boil. Add tomato puree, onions, carrots, and turnip. Let boil for 45 minutes. Add all remaining vegetables, salt, and crushed red pepper. Cook for 30 minutes. Break up vermicelli in soup. Let cook for 10 minutes. Yield: 6 to 8 servings.

GREEN SPLIT PEA SOUP

This soup I remember very well. Many times at Friday dinner, green split pea soup was served over rice with a potato and egg omelet, a biscuit, and strawberry jam. *C'est tout*—and eleven stomachs were filled!

1 lb. dried green split peas
2½ qt. water
1 cup chopped onions
¾ cup chopped celery
1 tsp. finely chopped garlic
½ cup chopped carrots
1½ tbsp. salt
½ tsp. white pepper
¼ lb. butter
1 cup evaporated milk

Remove all bad particles from peas. Wash and put peas in a 5-quart pot. Pour water over peas. Add onions, celery, and garlic. Bring to a hard boil, then lower heat. Cook over medium heat until peas are tender. Remove from heat. Process in blender until creamy. Return to pot. Add carrots, salt, white pepper, and butter; simmer for about 15 minutes. Stir in milk and let simmer for an additional 5 minutes. Yield: 6 servings.

YELLOW SPLIT PEA SOUP

1 lb. yellow split peas
2½ qt. water
1 cup chopped onions
½ cup chopped celery
1 tbsp. salt
½ cup margarine
½ lb. smoked sausage
    (thinly sliced)
1 tsp. chopped garlic
1 tsp. white pepper
½ tsp. cayenne pepper

Put split peas to boil in water with onions, celery, and salt. Let cook until peas are soft. Melt margarine in skillet and add smoked sausage. Stir sausage in margarine, cooking over medium heat for 3 minutes. Lower heat; let sausage simmer a little.

With a wire whisk, whip peas well (this makes them creamy). Add sausage and all sausage drippings to peas. Add garlic, white and cayenne peppers. If much of the water has boiled out of the peas, you should add a little more. Let soup simmer for 10 minutes. Yield: 6 servings.

MIRLITON SOUP

2 lb. mirlitons
2 qt. water
¼ lb. butter
1 cup chopped onions
¼ cup chopped celery
¼ cup all-purpose flour
¼ lb. smoked ham (finely
    chopped)
½ lb. shrimp (finely
    chopped)
1 clove garlic (finely
    chopped)
¼ tsp. ground thyme
½ pt. half-and-half
1 tbsp. chopped parsley
1 tbsp. salt
½ tsp. white pepper

Place mirlitons in pot with 2 quarts of water. Bring to boil and cook until tender. Remove mirlitons from pot; reserve water. With a small spoon, remove the pulp from the mirlitons and mash well, then set aside. Melt butter, add onions and celery. Cook until onions are clear. Stir in flour (do not brown) and cook for 5 minutes. Add ham and shrimp. Stir and cook for 5 minutes longer.

Return the reserved water to the mixture, stirring well (best to use a wire whisk). Add mirliton, garlic, and thyme. Whisk thoroughly. Add half-and-half, parsley, salt, and white pepper. Let simmer for 20 minutes. Yield: 6 servings.

POTATO SOUP

3 qt. water
3 lb. white potatoes (peeled)
½ cup chopped onions
½ cup chopped celery
¼ cup chopped green
   pepper
½ cup chopped green onions
1 tsp. chopped garlic
2 tbsp. chopped parsley
¼ lb. margarine
1 tbsp. salt
¼ tsp. thyme
1 whole red pepper

In a 5-quart stockpot, put water, potatoes, onions, celery, and green pepper. Bring to a hard boil. Lower heat and let boil slowly for 35 minutes or until potatoes are very soft. The potatoes should begin to break up! Once the potatoes are soft, take a wire whisk or potato masher and cream the potatoes. Personally, I like the mixture to be a little lumpy. Add the green onions, garlic, and parsley. Stir well. Lower the heat again and add salt, thyme, and whole red pepper. Let simmer for another 20 minutes. Stir well. Remove the whole red pepper. Add the margarine, constantly stirring. Great with garlic bread. Yield: 6 servings.

OKRA GUMBO

Okra gumbo or crowder peas were the big thing when I was growing up. Those would be your main dish. If you got fried chicken, that was actually considered the side dish.

> ¼ cup vegetable oil
> 3 lb. fresh okra (sliced thin)
> 3 medium blue crabs
> 1½ cups chopped onions
> ½ cup chopped green
>   pepper
> ½ cup chopped celery
> 2 tbsp. tomato paste
> 1½ qt. water
> 1 tsp. crushed red pepper
> ½ tsp. cayenne pepper
> 1 tsp. paprika
> 1 tsp. chopped garlic
> ½ tsp. whole thyme
> 1 tbsp. salt
> 2 bay leaves
> 1 lb. shrimp (cleaned and
>   deveined)

For this recipe, a heavy pot is needed (I use Magnalite). Heat the pot. Add oil and okra. Heat must not be high, as the okra must cook slowly. Stir the okra often, cooking for 20 minutes. Add the crabs, onions, green pepper, and celery. Cook for another 15 minutes. Give this pot a lot of attention or the okra will stick. Okra should be soft (not fried to a crisp). Add tomato paste and stir well. Slowly add the water. Stir in crushed red pepper, cayenne pepper, paprika, garlic, thyme, salt, and bay leaves. Cook for 10 minutes, then add the shrimp and continue cooking for another 10 minutes. Serve over rice. Yield: 4-6 servings.

GUMBO DES HERBES

1 bunch mustard greens
1 bunch collard greens
1 bunch turnips
1 bunch watercress
1 bunch beet tops
1 bunch carrot tops
½ head lettuce
½ head cabbage
1 bunch spinach
2 medium onions (chopped)
4 cloves garlic (mashed and
   chopped)
Water
1 lb. smoked sausage
1 lb. smoked ham
1 lb. chaurice (hot)
1 lb. brisket stew meat
1 lb. boneless brisket
5 tbsp. flour
1 tsp. thyme leaves
1 tbsp. salt
1 tsp. cayenne pepper
1 tbsp. filé powder

Clean all vegetables, making sure to pick out bad leaves and rinse away all grit. In a large pot place all greens, onions, and garlic. Cover with water and boil for 30 minutes. While this is boiling, cut all meats and sausages into bite-size pieces and set aside. Strain vegetables after boiling and reserve liquid. In a 12-quart stockpot place brisket meats, ham, smoked sausage, and 2 cups reserved liquid and steam for 15 minutes. While steaming place chaurice in skillet and steam until chaurice is rendered (all grease cooked out). Drain chaurice, keeping the grease in the skillet, and set aside.

All vegetables must be pureed. This can be done in a food processor or by hand in a meat grinder. Heat the skillet of chaurice grease and stir in flour. Cook roux for 5 minutes or until flour is cooked (does not have to brown). Pour roux over meat mixture; stir well. Add vegetables and 2 quarts reserved liquid. Let simmer for 20 minutes. Add chaurice, thyme, salt, and cayenne pepper; stir well. Simmer for 40 minutes. Add filé powder; stir well and remove from heat. Serve over steamed rice. Yield: 8 servings.

CREOLE GUMBO

This is a dish that always preceded any festive meal, or Sunday dinner for that matter. Every woman took pride in her gumbo making. I can remember, as a youngster, the care that went into gumbo making—how the crabs and shrimp were cleaned on Saturday and placed overnight in the icebox.

On Sunday morning, we rose early to attend Mass (in those days, Sunday Mass was in the mornings). Once back home, Sunday clothes were taken off and neatly hung up. Hats (as they were a must for women at Mass then) were put back into the armoire. Then, in less formal clothes, it was off to the kitchen. But before the gumbo making began, a cup of coffee and a hot calas (rice doughnut) or a biscuit was served.

Then, every female who was old enough helped prepare the Sunday meal. The aroma of crabs frying filled the house. Chicken necks and gizzards were cleaned and cut up along with sausages, ham, and chicken wings. It seemed that veal stew, for whatever reason, was also a must. My job was cutting onions and the other seasonings. My mother always made the roux, which took extreme care to get it just right.

4 hard-shell crabs, cleaned
½ lb. Creole hot sausage
  (cut in bite-size pieces)
½ lb. smoked sausage (cut
  in bite-size pieces)
½ lb. boneless veal stew
  meat
½ lb. chicken gizzards
½ cup vegetable oil
4 tbsp. flour
1 cup chopped onion
4 qt. water
6 chicken wings (cut in half)
½ lb. chicken necks
  (skinned and cut)
½ lb. smoked ham (cubed)
1 lb. shrimp (peeled and
  deveined)
1 tbsp. paprika
1 tsp. salt
3 cloves garlic (chopped
  fine)
¼ cup chopped parsley
1 tsp. ground thyme
24 oysters with their liquid
1 tbsp. filé powder

Put crabs, sausages, stew meat, and gizzards in 6-quart pot over medium heat. Cover and let cook in its own fat for 30 minutes (it will produce enough, but continue to watch the pot). Heat oil in skillet and add flour to make a roux. Stir constantly until very brown. Lower heat, add onions, and cook over low heat until onions wilt. Pour onion mixture over the ingredients in the large pot. Slowly add water, stirring constantly. Bring to a boil. Add chicken wings, necks, ham, shrimp, paprika, salt, garlic, parsley, and thyme. Let simmer for 30 minutes. Add oysters and liquid; cook for 10 minutes longer. Remove from heat; add filé powder, stirring well. Serve over rice. Yield: 8-10 servings.

Magnolia Side by Gilbert D. Fletcher

You have to be yourself when you are creating and cooking. You do what you know and do it to the best of your ability. I do some different things occasionally. I do cream sauces sometimes, but that is not what Dooky Chase's is all about. When you come to our restaurant, you know what you want.

Our recipes are not representative of "Uptown" New Orleans. They are just representative of the Chase family. So here are some sauce recipes that can complement many of the traditional Creole dishes, or anything else suitable!

HORSERADISH SAUCE

1 tsp. sugar
¼ tsp. salt
¼ tsp. white pepper
2 tbsp. vinegar
½ tsp. yellow mustard
¼ cup horseradish
1½ cups heavy cream

Mix all dry ingredients well. Add vinegar, mustard, and horseradish; whisk well. Whip in cream. Voilà …. Excellent on boiled beef or short ribs. Yield: about 2 cups.

EGG SAUCE

2 tbsp. butter
2 tbsp. flour
1½ cups milk
4 hard-boiled eggs
   (chopped)
1 tbsp. lemon juice
½ tsp. Tabasco sauce
½ tsp. salt
1 tsp. chopped parsley

In a saucepot, melt butter and add flour. Cook for 5 minutes, stirring often. Add milk and whisk well for smooth texture. Add eggs, lemon juice, Tabasco, salt, and parsley. Stir well. Great over poached fish. Yield: 2 cups.

LEAH'S BORDELAISE SAUCE

1 soup bone with marrow
  (ask your butcher)
1 carrot
½ onion
1 rib celery
2 qt. water
¼ lb. butter
1 tsp. flour
1 tbsp. chopped onion
1 tbsp. chopped garlic
½ cup burgundy wine
1 tsp. chopped celery leaves
1 tsp. salt
½ tsp. cayenne pepper

In a 5-quart stockpot put soup bone to boil with carrot, half of onion, celery rib, and 2 quarts of water. Let boil for 1 hour. Remove bone and reserve stock. With a knife, scrape marrow from bone and reserve. In a 2-quart stockpot, melt butter over medium heat. Add flour and stir well. Cook for 3 minutes.

Add chopped onions and cook until soft. Add finely chopped bone marrow; stir well. Add garlic. Add burgundy and stir well. Add 2 cups of reserved stock. With a wire whisk, stir briskly. Add celery leaves, salt, and cayenne, and stir well. Let simmer for 15 minutes. Serve over steaks or chops. Sauce can be stored in refrigerator for later use. Yield: 1½ gallons.

RICH CREAM SAUCE FOR FISH

½ cup butter
¼ cup flour
1 13-oz. can evaporated
   milk
½ cup water
3 eggs (well beaten)
½ tsp. salt
¼ tsp. cayenne pepper
½ tsp. Worcestershire
   sauce

Melt butter in saucepan. Add flour, stirring briskly (better to use a wire whisk). Cook over medium heat about 4 minutes. Slowly add milk, constantly stirring. Add water. Continue to stir mixture briskly to avoid lumping. Mixture should begin to thicken. Stir until smooth.

Take 2 tablespoons of the mixture and add to the beaten eggs. Beat well. Add this to mixture in saucepan, stirring briskly. Add salt, cayenne pepper, and Worcestershire sauce. Cook until smooth, about 5 minutes. Yield: 1 pint.

TARTARE SAUCE

1 pt. mayonnaise
½ cup chopped dill pickles
¼ cup chopped green
   onions
3 tbsp. chopped capers
1 tbsp. lemon juice
¼ tsp. cayenne pepper

Mix all ingredients well. Serve over fried seafood. Yield: 1½ pints.

DOOKY SAUCE

2 tbsp. horseradish
2 tbsp. yellow mustard
2 tbsp. ketchup
1 tsp. paprika
1 tbsp. chopped garlic
2 tbsp. chopped celery
2 cups vegetable oil
1 cup vinegar
½ tsp. salt

In a quart container, place all ingredients and shake well. Chill. This sauce can be poured over boiled shrimp or crab meat. Can be stored in refrigerator for later use. Yield: 1½ pints.

CREOLE MUSTARD SAUCE

1 tbsp. butter
1 tbsp. flour
2 cups milk
3 tbsp. Creole mustard
1 tbsp. vinegar
1 tsp. sugar

In a skillet, heat butter. Add flour and mix well. Add milk and cook until milk thickens. Add mustard and vinegar. Stir in sugar and cook for 5 minutes. Excellent on fish. Yield: 1 pint.

COCKTAIL SAUCE

1 cup ketchup
2 tbsp. lemon juice
1 tbsp. Worcestershire
  sauce
1 heaping tbsp. horseradish
1 tsp. chopped green
  onions
1 tsp. chopped green
  pepper
½ tsp. Tabasco sauce

In a quart container, place all ingredients and shake well. Chill. Can be used as a dip for boiled shrimp or raw oysters. This sauce can be stored in refrigerator for later use. Yield: 1 pint.

CUSTARD SAUCE

2 cups milk
2 eggs (beaten)
2 tbsp. sugar
½ tsp. vanilla

Place milk in top of double boiler. Get the milk very hot but not boiling. Mix the eggs and sugar together. Whisking the milk, add the egg mixture very slowly. Use a rubber spatula to remove all of the egg from the bowl. Blend well and cook over boiling water, whisking constantly. Custard should coat the back of spoon when cooked enough. Remove from heat and stir in vanilla. Use on desserts. Yield: 1 pint.

BREAD SAUCE

¼ cup butter
¼ cup chopped onions
1 tbsp. chopped celery
2 cups Pet milk
¼ cup water
¾ cup bread crumbs
½ tsp. salt
½ tsp. white pepper
½ tsp. allspice
½ tsp. chopped parsley
Cheese croutons

Melt butter in medium saucepot. Add onions and celery. Cook until onions are clear. Slowly add Pet milk and water. Bring to a slow boil. Stir well. Add bread crumbs and stir well. Add salt, white pepper, and allspice; simmer for 5 minutes. Add chopped parsley and cheese croutons. Serve over roast chicken or Cornish hens. Yield: 1½ pints.

COFFEE SAUCE

4 egg yolks (beaten)
3 tbsp. sugar
2 cups black coffee
2 tbsp. Pet milk
2 tbsp. Kahlua

In a small saucepot, mix eggs and sugar together. Slowly whisk in coffee and milk. Cook over medium heat until sauce coats back of spoon. Stir in Kahlua and remove from heat. Use on puddings or ice cream. Yield: 1 to 1½ cups.

CHOCOLATE SAUCE

1 cup sugar
¼ cup water
2 oz. unsweetened chocolate
2 tbsp. chocolate liqueur
1 tsp. butter

In a small saucepot, mix sugar with water. Grate the unsweetened chocolate into the sugar mixture. Bring mixture to boil and let boil for 5 to 6 minutes. Add liqueur and stir well. Whisk in butter and remove from heat. Yield: 1 cup.

BOURBON SAUCE

3 tbsp. butter
1 tbsp. flour
½ cup sugar
1 cup cream
1 tbsp. vanilla
1 tsp. nutmeg
1 oz. bourbon

In a small saucepot, melt butter and flour and cook for 5 minutes. Stir in sugar; add cream. Cook for 3 minutes. Add vanilla, nutmeg, and bourbon. Let simmer for 5 minutes. Yield: 1½ cups.

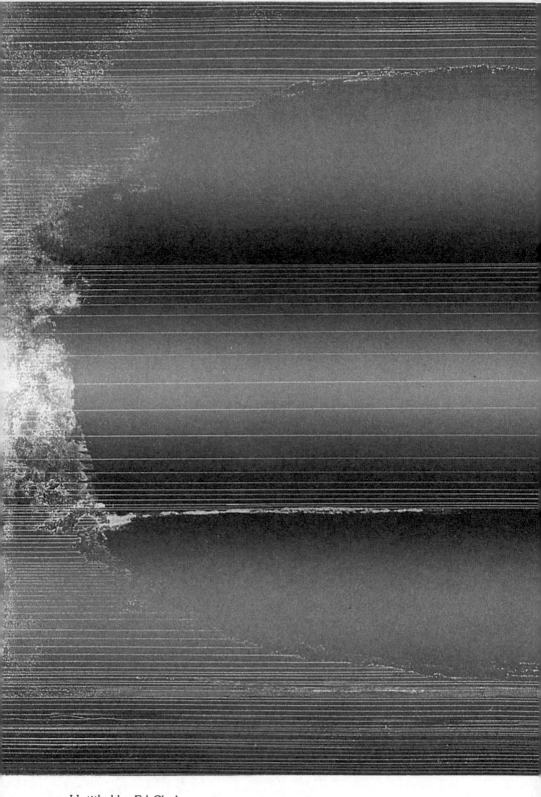

Untitled by Ed Clark

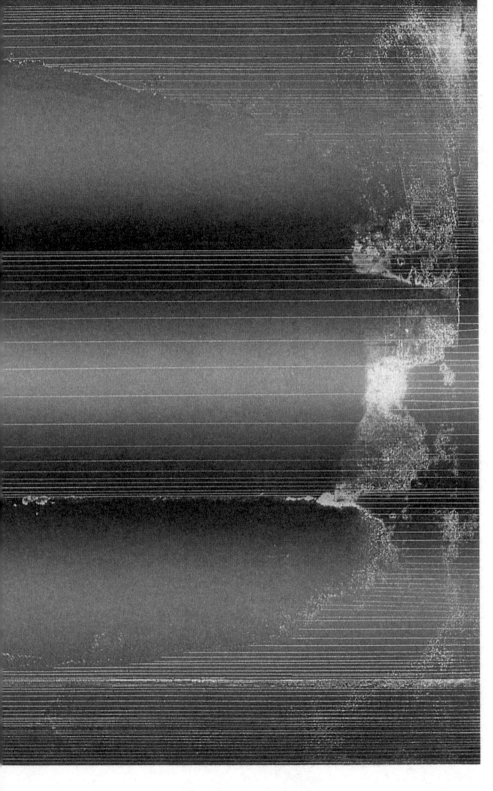

My mother was the fisherman in our family. She loved it so. She would get up early, particularly on Saturdays, and yell, "Put the grits on, I am going to get the fish." I don't know how many times we had grits without the fish. I love fish and grits still today.

My mother could fish all day. She might be in the middle of sewing and would get tired, then go dig herself a can of worms and get to the fishpond. That really caused her death, sitting on a fishpond. A man was passing in his motorboat one day and the boat threw water up on the bank and got Mother soaking wet. You think she would stop fishing? No, she sat there and kept on. After that she got pneumonia and she never got well. If you go there now, her tomb is right near her fishing spot.

I can eat fish everyday. I like good food, preparing it and eating it. This section on seafood dishes will let you in on the way I do it at Dooky Chase's.

TOMATO STUFFED WITH SHRIMP

4 medium tomatoes
½ stick butter
**½ cup chopped green
  onions**
**1 lb. shrimp (peeled,
  deveined, and chopped)**
1 tsp. salt
½ tsp. cayenne pepper
**2 fresh sweet basil leaves
  (chopped)**
½ cup bread crumbs
Butter for tops

Wash and cut tops from tomatoes. With a teaspoon, remove inside from tomatoes. Place pulp in bowl. Place tomatoes in small glass baking dish.

Melt butter in pot. Add chopped green onions and shrimp; cook for 5 minutes. Add insides from tomatoes, mashing well into shrimp mixture. Add salt, cayenne pepper, and basil. Cook for 10 minutes. Sir the mixture, sort of chopping tomatoes as they are cooking. Tighten mixture with some of the bread crumbs. Stuff tomatoes with shrimp mixture and sprinkle tops with remaining bread crumbs and dot with butter. Bake in 375-degree oven for about 10 minutes. Do not overcook or tomatoes will fall. Yield: 4 servings.

SHRIMP SALAD

Water
Salt to taste
1 lemon wedge
Cayenne pepper
3 tbsp. liquid crab boil
2 lb. shrimp
3 hard-boiled eggs (cubed)
½ cup coarsely chopped
celery
½ cup extra-virgin olive oil
¼ cup vinegar
1 tbsp. chopped parsley
6 to 8 pitted ripe olives
(cut in half)
Lettuce leaf
Sliced tomatoes and
cucumbers for garnish

Fill a 5-quart stockpot three-fourths full with water. Add salt, lemon wedge, cayenne pepper, and crab boil; bring to boil. Wash shrimp and add to boiling mixture. Boil shrimp for 10 minutes. Drain off water and let cool. Peel and devein shrimp. Cut shrimp into pieces. Toss shrimp with eggs, celery, oil, vinegar, parsley, and olives. Let chill for about 1 hour. Serve on lettuce leaf and garnish with sliced tomatoes and cucumbers. Yield: 4 servings.

FRIED SHRIMP

In the summertime, people would come around on trucks selling shrimp and oysters. We were always happy for that, because we did not have shrimp and oysters in the country very often. My mother had a way of cooking those shrimp that was so good. If she was ironing clothes when the man came around, she just washed the shrimp, rolled them in cornmeal, and fried them on that iron skillet in the shell—head and all. The recipe below, although the shrimp are peeled, is just as good.

2 lb. shrimp
1 egg (beaten)
1 can Pet milk
4 cups vegetable oil
2 cups corn flour or fish fry
2 tsp. salt
2 tsp. black pepper

Peel and devein shrimp. Wash shrimp and pat dry. Mix beaten egg and milk together well. Soak shrimp in mixture for 5 minutes.

In a Magnalite chicken fryer, pour oil, place on medium heat, and bring temperature of oil to 360 degrees. Mix corn flour and salt and pepper. Remove shrimp from milk mixture (several at a time) and place in corn flour, coating well. Shake shrimp to remove excess corn flour.

Gently place shrimp in hot oil. Fry for 5 minutes. Remove shrimp and drain on paper towels. Yield: 4 servings.

SHRIMP CLEMENCEAU

1 stick butter
2 medium potatoes (peeled
  and diced small)
2 lb. small shrimp (peeled
  and deveined)
2 cloves garlic (finely
  chopped)
½ cup button mushrooms
1 cup green peas
¼ tsp. chopped fresh
  parsley
⅓ cup white wine
Salt and pepper

Melt butter in 2-quart saucepan. Add potatoes. Cook 5 minutes.
Add shrimp, garlic, and mushrooms. Cook until shrimp are tender.
Add peas, parsley, and wine. Salt and pepper to taste. Cook for 5
minutes. Yield: 4 servings.

FRIED FISH SALAD

Cold leftover fried fish
Italian dressing
Chopped cucumbers
Finely chopped red onions
Capers
Mayonnaise
Lettuce leaf

This was always a good way of utilizing leftover fried fish. Take the cold fried fish and cut into bite-size cubes. Pour Italian dressing over fish. Refrigerate for about 1 hour or even overnight. Drain fish and add chopped cucumbers, finely chopped red onions, a few capers, and just enough mayonnaise to hold the salad together. Toss lightly, being careful not to break up fish. Serve on lettuce leaf.

BAKED FISH WITH ARTICHOKES AND CHEESE

6 medium trout or catfish
fillets
Juice of 1 lemon
Salt and pepper to taste
2 tbsp. chopped parsley
14 oz. artichoke hearts
(drained and mashed)
1 pt. mayonnaise
4 oz. grated mozzarella
cheese
3 tbsp. grated Parmesan
cheese

Preheat oven to 350 degrees. Wash and dry fillets; lay flat in an 8½" x 12" baking dish. Pour lemon juice over fish, season, and add parsley. Layer artichokes, mayonnaise, mozzarella, and Parmesan cheese over the fish. Bake 30 to 45 minutes or until fish flakes with fork. Yield: 6 servings.

WHOLE BOILED RED SNAPPER

This was a must at all festive occasions in my childhood, especially Thanksgiving and Christmas dinner. In the old days, red snapper was not hard to come by.

"Making market" (the term used for going to the market) for holiday cooking was a very special event. One always had a nice cane basket with a cover. Always noticeable were stalks of celery and the tail of a red snapper protruding from the basket.

The fish was cleaned, prepared, and garnished with care. Along with fresh stalks of celery, this made a beautiful edible centerpiece for the table.

1 5-lb. red snapper
Water to cover
1 tbsp. salt
½ tsp. cayenne pepper
2 bay leaves
2 tbsp. liquid crab boil
2 ribs celery
2 cups mayonnaise
1 tsp. dillweed
Green lettuce leaves
1 cup chopped celery
¼ cup chopped green
**   onions**
1 cup chopped green olives
2 hard-boiled eggs
1 tbsp. chopped parsley
Lemon and tomato wedge
**   for garnish**

Place fish in cheesecloth and put in a fish poacher or deep pan. Cover with water and add salt, cayenne pepper, bay leaves, crab boil, and celery ribs. Bring water to a boil and boil for 20 to 30 minutes. Remove the fish from the water and let cool.

Mix mayonnaise with dillweed and refrigerate for 10 minutes. Line a large platter with green lettuce leaves. Remove the fish from the cheesecloth and place on the platter. Sprinkle chopped celery, green onions, and olives over entire fish. Spread mayonnaise mixture over fish. Slice the eggs and arrange over mayonnaise. Sprinkle with parsley. Garnish around fish with lemon and tomato wedges. Yield: 6 to 8 servings as a side dish.

CODFISH BALLS

1 lb. dry salted codfish
Water to cover
2 medium white potatoes
  (boiled)
2 tbsp. chopped green
  onions
1 tsp. white pepper
1 tsp. chopped parsley
¼ cup Pet milk
2 eggs (beaten)
1½ cups flour
2 cups vegetable oil

Boil fish in enough water to cover. Cook until flaky. Drain fish and remove all bones if any. Peel potatoes and mash with fish. Add green onions, white pepper, parsley, milk, and beaten eggs. Mix well. Shape into balls, then with the palm of the hand flatten a bit. Dust all sides with flour.

Heat oil in heavy skillet. Place fish balls in hot oil and brown on both sides. Cook about 5 minutes. Drain off all fat. Place on hot platter. Yield: 6 balls.

COURT BOUILLON

1 4- to 5-lb. redfish (or any
   other firm fish)
1 bay leaf
Celery
Carrots
Onions
Garlic
½ cup vegetable oil
2 tbsp. flour
½ cup chopped onions
½ cup chopped green
   peppers
1 tbsp. chopped garlic
3 cups whole tomatoes
1 tsp. whole thyme leaves
1 tbsp. salt
½ tsp. cayenne pepper
1 whole red pepper
1 tbsp. chopped parsley

Scale and gut fish. Remove fish from bones, saving head and bones. Cut each side of fish in three pieces. (You may have the market clean and prepare fish. Ask for bones and head.)

In large pot, put head and bones to boil with bay leaf, celery, carrots, onions, and garlic. Pour stock off through sieve and save. In Magnalite Dutch oven, heat oil. Add flour and cook to a light tan. Add onions and cook until they are clear. Add green pepper and garlic. Continue to stir.

Add whole tomatoes and 3 cups fish stock. Stir well. Add thyme, salt, cayenne pepper, whole red pepper, and parsley. Let gravy come to boil; lower heat.

Add fish. Simmer for 20 minutes until fish flakes. Serve over rice. Yield: 4 to 6 servings.

FISHERMAN'S PIE

3 cups mashed potatoes
½ lb. cod
3 cups water
½ lb. catfish
½ lb. shrimp (peeled and
    deveined)
1 cup white crab meat
¼ cup butter
2 tbsp. flour
1 cup Pet milk
½ tsp. salt
1 tsp. Tabasco sauce
1 tbsp. Worcestershire sauce
1 tbsp. parsley
½ cup grated cheddar cheese

Press 2 cups of the mashed potatoes in a 9-inch glass pie plate to form a pie shell. In saucepot, place cod, cover with the water, and bring to a boil. Lower heat and simmer for 5 minutes. Add catfish and shrimp and continue to simmer until catfish flakes and shrimp are about done. Drain off stock and reserve. Flake fish; add crab meat to seafood. Place seafood mixture in potato shell and set aside.

Melt butter in skillet. Add flour and stir constantly—do not brown. Add milk and ½ cup reserved fish stock. Whisk mixture until smooth and creamy. Add salt, Tabasco, Worcestershire, and parsley; mix well. Pour sauce over seafood mixture, covering all of the fish. Place remaining potatoes in a pastry bag. Pipe ring of potatoes around pie. Make a rosette in middle of pie. Sprinkle entire pie with grated cheddar cheese. Bake in 375-degree oven for 40 minutes or until pie is golden. Yield: 6 servings.

FLOUNDER
STUFFED WITH CRAB MEAT

Dooky Chase's was my mother-in-law's whole life, but she didn't know how to grow in the restaurant. She wasn't the type to go out and seek change, but the place would suffer for it. I go out to see what other restaurants have and see if I can do that too. I learn as I go. You grow as you go to different places and read books. I learned that flounder is just a lemon sole. You look at what they do with sole and apply that to flounder and your mind is turning. You can roll the fillet, or bang it out and stuff it with crab meat. This recipe for flounder stuffed with crab meat is simply a result of me playing around with the possibilities, and using what's on hand.

4 1- to 1½-lb. flounders
Salt and black pepper
1 lb. white crab meat
3 tbsp. vegetable oil
½ cup chopped onions
½ cup chopped celery
1 tbsp. chopped parsley
2 cloves garlic (finely
**   chopped)**
1 tsp. salt
½ tsp. cayenne pepper
1 tsp. paprika
½ tsp. thyme leaves
1 egg (beaten)
½ cup seasoned bread
**   crumbs**
Butter

Remove scales and entrails from flounder. Cut off heads just behind the gills. Wash fish well. Place on board and with a sharp knife make a slit down the top of the flounder. Raise flesh from bones, careful not to cut through the sides. Remove bones and wash cavities. Season fish with salt and black pepper and set aside.

Go through crab meat, removing any shell particles; set aside. In a heavy saucepan, heat the oil. Add the onions and celery. Sauté until tender. Add crab meat to onion mixture. Add parsley, garlic, salt, cayenne pepper, paprika, and thyme. Continue to stir and cook for 15 minutes on medium heat. Add beaten egg; stir in mixture. Tighten with bread crumbs.

Fill fish cavities with crab meat dressing. Place fish in greased baking pan. Brush with butter. Bake in 375-degree oven for 45 minutes or until fish are flaky. Yield: 4 servings.

FLOUNDER FILLETS
IN BUTTER SAUCE

---

6 flounder fillets
½ tsp. salt
½ tsp. white pepper
¼ cup butter
½ cup white wine
1 tbsp. Worcestershire
   sauce
1 tsp. Tabasco sauce
2 tbsp. lemon juice
1 tbsp. chopped parsley

Pat fish fillets dry with paper towels. Season fish with salt and white pepper. Spray baking dish with nonstick cooking spray. Loosely roll each fillet and place in baking dish. Drizzle fillets with 1 teaspoon of butter. Bake for 25 minutes in a 350-degree oven or until fish is white and flaky. In a skillet slightly brown remaining butter; add wine, Worcestershire, Tabasco, and lemon juice. Simmer on low heat for 10 minutes. Pour over fish fillets. Garnish with chopped parsley. Yield: 6 servings.

PAN-FRIED FLOUNDER

In 1946 I was on the road with my husband Dooky and his band. He had twin vocalists from Mobile in the band. After a long bus ride from Miami, we stopped at the home of the twins. Musicians were always starving in those days, so we showed up with quite an appetite. The twins' mother had just caught about six big flounder out of Mobile Bay. She prepared them in just this fashion. I thought it was the best-tasting fish—unless I was just starving!

1 3-lb. flounder
1 cup flour
1 cup cornmeal
1 tbsp. salt
1 tbsp. white pepper
1 tsp. paprika
1 pt. vegetable oil

Properly clean fish; remove head. Cut fish crosswise into 2-inch strips. In a bowl, mix flour and cornmeal well. Add salt, white pepper, and paprika; mix well. Roll fish in cornmeal mixture, coating well. In a heavy frying pan, heat oil. Place fish in hot oil and brown on both sides; this takes about 5 to 6 minutes' frying time. Yield: 4 servings.

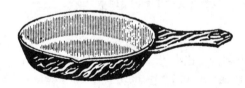

BAKED REDFISH
OR SHEEPHEAD

1 4-lb. redfish or
   sheephead
Salt and black pepper
1 lemon
2 tbsp. vegetable oil
1 tbsp. flour
1 onion (chopped)
1 green pepper (chopped)
1 6-oz. can tomato paste
4 cups water
½ tsp. cayenne pepper
1 tsp. chopped garlic
1 tbsp. chopped parsley
½ tsp. oregano leaves
1 bay leaf
1 tbsp. liquid crab boil
Chopped green onions for
   garnish

Fish should be scaled and gutted. Do not remove head. Wash fish well, cleaning the cavity of all blood. Rub fish in and out with salt and pepper. Squeeze lemon over fish. Place in baking pan—set aside.

In a 3-quart saucepot, heat the oil over medium heat. Add flour, stirring and cooking until flour is slightly brown. Add onions and cook for 3 minutes. Add green pepper and tomato paste. Stir well or paste will stick. Slowly add the water, stirring until mixture is without lumps. Add cayenne pepper, garlic, parsley, oregano, bay leaf, and crab boil. Cook slowly for 25 minutes.

Pour over fish and bake in preheated 350-degree oven for 1 hour. Try fish for doneness

Place on platter, spooning sauce over and around fish. Garnish with chopped green onions. Yield: 6 servings.

REDFISH ORLEANS

3 tbsp. butter
2 cups water
¼ tsp. cayenne pepper
1 tsp. salt
4 6-oz. redfish fillets
1 tbsp. flour
½ cup Pet milk
¼ cup white wine
1 tbsp. Worcestershire
  sauce
White pepper
2 cups lump white crab meat
Parsley and lemon for
  garnish

In a large pan, place 1 tablespoon of the butter and the 2 cups of water. Bring water to boil. Add cayenne pepper and 1 teaspoon salt to water. Place fish in boiling water and poach until fish is cooked, about 10 minutes. Remove fish from water; place on platter and keep warm. Reserve liquid.

Melt remaining butter in pot. Add flour; stir well. Do not brown. Add milk, stirring with a wire whisk to keep it smooth. Slowly add wine and reserved liquid. Whisk briskly until smooth; add Worcestershire and a little white pepper. Add crab meat to sauce and simmer for 3 minutes. Pour over fish fillets. Garnish with parsley and lemon. Yield: 4 servings.

SALMON CROQUETTES

Some of my recipes call for canned salmon instead of fresh because that was the only way we were able to buy it in the country. We didn't have fresh salmon in the ponds or stores in Madisonville. This salmon croquettes recipe is always a winner.

1-lb. can pink salmon
2 tbsp. butter
2 tbsp. flour
¼ cup finely chopped
onions
1 cup Pet milk
1 egg (beaten)
1 cup bread crumbs
2 cups vegetable oil
1 tsp. chopped parsley

Drain and save liquid from salmon. Empty can and remove skin and bones; set aside. Melt butter in saucepot. Add flour. Stir well but do not brown flour. Add onions and continue to cook for a few minutes. Slowly add milk and continue to stir. A wire whisk works well here. Mixture must be smooth. Add beaten egg; whisk well. Add about ½ cup liquid from salmon. Mix well. Flake salmon into sauce and add parsley. Stir well. Pour into glass bowl. Refrigerate for 1 hour.

Remove from refrigerator and shape mixture into pyramids. Roll each one in bread crumbs. Heat oil. Fry croquettes until brown on all sides. Yield: 6 croquettes.

SALMON SALAD

1-lb. can pink salmon
1 red onion (thinly sliced)
½ cup salad oil
¼ cup vinegar
½ tsp. salt
½ tsp. black pepper
¼ tsp. paprika

Remove salmon from can; drain off liquid and discard. Remove all bones and skin. Place salmon in glass bowl. Add sliced onions.

In a bowl mix oil, vinegar, salt, pepper, and paprika. Pour over salmon. Toss gently. Refrigerate for 30 minutes. Serve on lettuce leaf. Yield: 4 servings.

GRILLED SALMON STEAKS WITH GREEN PEPPERCORNS

4 thick salmon steaks
Salt and pepper
2 tbsp. green peppercorns
   (in water)
2 tbsp. melted butter

Season steaks with salt and pepper. Squeeze peppercorns between fingers and rub over steaks, mashing them into the fish. Brush with butter. Place on hot grill. Turn from side to side until steaks are nice and flaky, about 15 minutes. Yield: 4 servings.

POACHED SALMON
WITH CHAMPAGNE SAUCE

2 8-oz. salmon fillets
2 cups water
Salt
White pepper
1 cup champagne

Cut each fillet in half lengthwise. Roll each strip and secure with toothpick. Put water in frying pan and let come to a boil. Add salt and white pepper. Place fillets in boiling water for 6 minutes; turn once but don't crumble the fish. When fillets are just about done add champagne. Let simmer until done, about 5 minutes. Yield: 4 servings.

OVEN-FRIED FISH FILLETS

1 cup fish fry or corn flour
½ tsp. paprika
4 6-oz. fish fillets
White pepper to taste

Mix fish fry with paprika; set aside. Wash fillets. Do not dry. Sprinkle white pepper on fish. Dredge fillets in fish fry mixture. Spray baking pan with nonstick cooking spray. Lay fillets flat in pan. Bake in preheated 375-degree oven for 30 minutes or until fish flake when pricked with a fork. Yield: 4 servings.

FRIED PERCH

When we were children, Mother would get up very early on Saturday mornings before her day's work. She headed for the bayou, with a cane pole in one hand and a can of worms in the other.

I never remembered my mother needing a Valium or any relaxer. With eleven of us you would think she would be driven up the wall half the time ... but never. That fishing pole was her relaxer. She loved to catch those little perch. If she caught a sacalait, which is a nice larger perch with the sweetest meat ever, you would think she had gold.

Those perch and grits were our Saturday breakfast.

If you've never gone perch fishing, you've missed a great time. Take the kids ... we do it all the time. Just sit and wait for that cork to bob up and down. It's relaxing, a lot of fun, and costs nothing but a can of worms.

> **4 perch**
> **Salt**
> **Pepper**
> **1 pt. vegetable oil or 1 lb.**
> **   pork lard**
> **Corn flour or fish fry**

Clean perch. With a sharp knife, make one or two slits across the fish. Salt and pepper each fish.

Heat oil in frying pan. Shake fish in corn flour until they are well coated. Place fish in hot oil. Fry until lightly browned on each side. Yield: 4 servings.

FRIED TROUT FILLETS

6 4- to 6-oz. fillets
Salt and pepper
1 cup corn flour
2 cups vegetable oil

Season fish with salt and pepper. Shake fish in corn flour, coating well.

Heat oil in frying pan. Place fish in hot oil. Fry until golden on each side, about 10 minutes. Drain fish on paper towels. Serve with chilled potato salad. Yield: 6 servings.

GRILLED TROUT

Whole trout (scaled and
**   gutted)**
Salt and pepper
Whole dried red peppers
Sliced onions
Olive oil

You will need at least one 1½-pound trout per serving. Wash and wipe fish in and out. Season with salt and pepper. Fill cavity of each fish with dried red peppers and sliced onions. Close cavity. Brush outside of fish with olive oil. Grill fish over hot coals or an electric grill, turning twice. Brush oil over fish as they are cooking. This takes about 30 minutes. Test fish for flakiness.

TROUT AMANDINE

1 cup Pet milk
¼ cup water
1 egg (beaten)
6 6-oz. trout fillets
1 cup flour
1 tsp. salt
½ tsp. white pepper
¾ cup chopped almonds
1½ cups butter
Lemon wedges and parsley
    for garnish

Mix milk, water, and egg. Pour mixture over trout fillets. Let soak for about 5 minutes. Mix flour, salt, white pepper, and ½ cup of the chopped almonds. Take fillets and press them well in flour mixture. Make sure almonds stick firmly to fish.

Heat 1 cup of the butter in frying pan. Place fish in hot butter and cook until light brown on both sides. Be careful not to get butter too hot. Drain fish on paper towel. Add remaining butter and almonds to pan; simmer for 5 minutes.

Place fish on platter. Pour sautéed almonds over fish. Garnish with lemon wedges and parsley. Yield: 6 servings.

RAINBOW TROUT
WITH CRAWFISH MOUSSE

4 rainbow trout
Salt and pepper for fish
½ tsp. salt
1 tsp. white pepper
1 lb. crawfish tails
2 egg whites (unbeaten)
½ tsp. mace
2 cups heavy cream
2 tbsp. flour
1 cup white wine

Remove heads from fish. Take out bones, leaving both sides intact. Salt and pepper fish; set aside. Put crawfish in a bowl and mash well. Place bowl inside a larger bowl that has been filled with crushed ice. Pour egg whites over crawfish. Continue to mix, adding salt, white pepper, and mace. Mash well into crawfish mixture. Add cream and mix well. Mixture should be a smooth paste. Let sit in ice for 30 minutes to stiffen. Spoon mixture in each fish and fold loosely. Place fish in well-buttered baking dish. Dust flour over fish.

Pour wine around trout. Place in preheated 375-degree oven. Bake for 35 minutes, basting fish from time to time. Yield: 4 servings.

CRAWFISH ETOUFFEE

¼ cup margarine
2 tbsp. vegetable oil
2 tbsp. flour
¼ cup chopped onions
¼ cup chopped green
   peppers
¼ cup chopped celery
3 cloves garlic (chopped
   and mashed)
3 cups hot water
¼ cup chopped green
   onions
¼ tsp. whole thyme leaves
1 bay leaf
1 tbsp. salt
½ tsp. crushed red pepper
¼ tsp. cayenne pepper
1 lb. cooked crawfish tails
1 tbsp. chopped parsley

In a 3-quart heavy pot, heat margarine and vegetable oil. Add flour to hot oil, stirring constantly. Cook for 5 minutes.

Add onions, stirring as they cook. Add green peppers, celery, and garlic. Slowly add hot water. Mix well.

Add green onion, thyme, bay leaf, salt, crushed red pepper, and cayenne. Bring to a boil. Let simmer for 10 minutes.

Add crawfish tails and parsley. Cook about 5 minutes longer. Serve over steamed rice. Yield: 4 servings.

SOFT-SHELL CRABS WITH
CRAWFISH SAUCE

4 large soft-shell crabs
  (properly cleaned)
2 tsp. salt
1 tsp. white pepper
1 cup flour
⅓ cup butter
½ cup chopped onions
½ cup chopped green
  pepper
2 cups water
1 tbsp. paprika
1 tbsp. chopped garlic
½ tsp. cayenne pepper
1 lb. cooked crawfish tails
1 ripe avocado
2 tbsp. chopped parsley
Lemon for garnish

Season cleaned crabs with 1 teaspoon salt and 1 teaspoon white pepper. Dredge crabs in flour; set aside. Place butter in skillet; heat over medium heat, being careful not to burn. When butter is hot, shake off excess flour from crabs and place crabs in hot butter. Cook for 10 minutes, turning crabs as they cook. Remove from skillet; set aside.

To the skillet, add the remaining flour, stirring constantly over medium heat. Add onions and cook until onions are clear. Add green peppers and stir while cooking for 4 minutes. Add water slowly, constantly stirring. Add paprika, garlic, remaining salt, and cayenne pepper. Stir well. Raise the heat and bring sauce to a boil. Lower heat and simmer sauce for 5 minutes. Add crawfish tails. Cook 5 minutes more. Return crabs to crawfish mixture. Simmer for about 6 minutes, basting crabs with crawfish sauce.

Peel avocado and cut in four equal parts. Arrange on platter, placing one crab on each piece of avocado. Spoon crawfish sauce over crabs. Garnish with parsley and lemon. Yield: 4 servings.

BOILED CRAWFISH

10 lb. live crawfish
Cold water to cover
2 tbsp. salt
3 gallons water
1 cup liquid crab boil
2 bay leaves
1 tbsp. cayenne
1 whole lemon (cut in half)
1 small head garlic
½ lb. salt pork
4 ears corn (cut in half)
10 whole new potatoes

Place live crawfish in large pot of cold water—enough to cover. Add salt and let sit for 30 minutes. This will clear out some of the mud.

Place large stockpot on stove with 3 gallons of water. Place all seasonings plus corn in water and bring to a boil. Add crawfish and potatoes to boiling water. When crawfish begin to boil, cook for 15 minutes. Turn off heat and let sit for about 30 minutes. Drain water off. Let crawfish cool. Yield: 6 servings.

MOLDED CRAB MEAT SALAD

2 envelopes gelatin
1 cup cold water
½ tsp. salt
¼ tsp. cayenne pepper
½ tsp. yellow mustard
1 tbsp. lemon juice
¾ cup mayonnaise
½ cup chopped celery
6 ripe olives (sliced)
1 tsp. dillweed
1 tsp. chopped parsley
1 tsp. capers
1 lb. lump crab meat
Lettuce leaf and cucumbers
    for garnish

Mix gelatin in cup of cold water and dissolve well. Heat gelatin until all is dissolved. Remove from heat. Add salt, cayenne pepper, and mustard; let cool. Add lemon juice and put in refrigerator for 15 minutes. Beat in the mayonnaise and add celery, olives, dillweed, parsley, and capers. Gently toss in crab meat. Pour into a 3-cup mold. Let set until firm. Serve on lettuce leaf and garnish with cucumbers.

STUFFED CRABS

4 slices stale bread
2 cups water
1 lb. white crab meat
¼ cup vegetable oil
1 cup chopped onions
1 cup chopped celery
1½ tsp. salt
1 tsp. cayenne pepper
1 tsp. garlic
1 tbsp. parsley
1 tbsp. paprika
4 to 6 crab shells (glass or
    aluminum if real ones are
    unavailable)
Bread crumbs
Melted butter

Place bread in a deep dish. Pour water over bread and let soak until bread is a soft pulp. Set aside. Spread crab meat on pan. Pick all the shell particles from meat. Set aside.

In a heavy pot, heat oil. Add onions and celery; cook until onions are clear. Squeeze all excess water from bread and add bread to onion mixture. Stir well; add salt, cayenne, garlic, parsley, and paprika. Stir; cook for 30 minutes on medium heat. Make sure there are no lumps of bread; mixture should be smooth. Add crab meat and mix well. Cook for 10 minutes. Cool. If mixture is too loose, tighten to desired consistency with plain bread crumbs.

Wash and scrub crab shells. Boil to be sure they are perfectly clean. Let shells drain. Stuff mixture in high mounds into shells and sprinkle with bread crumbs. Drizzle with butter. Bake in 375-degree oven for 10 minutes. Yield: 4 to 6 servings.

OYSTERS AND SPAGHETTI

12-oz. pkg. of No. 4
  spaghetti
½ cup vegetable oil
3 tbsp. flour
1 onion (chopped)
¼ cup chopped celery
1 pt. oysters in liquid
½ cup water
1 tbsp. chopped garlic
1 tbsp. chopped parsley
1 tsp. salt
1 tsp. crushed red pepper
1 tsp. paprika
1 sprig thyme

Boil spaghetti until barely tender—*al dente*. Drain spaghetti and set aside.

Heat oil in saucepan. Add flour and cook until flour is light brown. Add onions and cook slowly until onions are clear. Add celery and liquid from oysters plus the water. Stir well. Add garlic, parsley, salt, crushed red pepper, paprika, and thyme. Let simmer for 10 minutes. Add oysters and simmer until oysters curl on ends, about 5 minutes. Pour over spaghetti. Heat in 375-degree oven for 10 minutes. Yield: 4 servings.

OYSTERS NORMAN

1 lb. fresh chopped spinach
(or 1 10-oz. pkg. frozen
chopped spinach)
½ stick butter
2 tbsp. flour
¼ cup chopped green
onions
1 tsp. chopped garlic
16 large oysters in liquid
1 cup water
½ tsp. salt
½ tsp. cayenne pepper
4 strips bacon
½ lb. shrimp
2 tbsp. chopped lettuce
¼ tsp. salt
¼ tsp. pepper
1 tbsp. Herbsaint
Bread crumbs

Boil spinach; drain; set aside. Heat butter in saucepan. Add flour, stirring constantly, and cook for 5 minutes. Add green onions and garlic; continue to stir. Add water from oysters plus 1 cup of water. Let simmer for 10 minutes on a slow heat. Add the ½ teaspoon of salt and the cayenne.

Add oysters; cook for 3 minutes until oysters curl. Place oysters on four coquilles (shell dishes). Set aside. Place bacon strips in frying pan and cook until crisp. Drain on paper towels. Chop shrimp and add to bacon drippings; stir. Cook for 3 or 4 minutes until shrimp are pink. Add chopped spinach, lettuce, the ¼ teaspoon of salt, and the pepper. Add Herbsaint. Stir and cook for 2 or 3 minutes.

Spoon spinach mixture over oysters. Sprinkle bread crumbs over each filled shell. Crumble bacon over bread crumbs. Bake for 10 minutes in 375-degree oven. Yield: 4 servings.

OYSTER PATTIES

1 tbsp. vegetable oil
1 tbsp. flour
1 medium onion (chopped)
¼ cup chopped celery
2 cloves garlic (chopped
    fine)
1 tsp. chopped parsley
½ tsp. salt
½ tsp. cayenne pepper
½ tsp. paprika
1 pt. oysters in liquid
1 cup water
6 medium patty shells

Heat oil. Add flour while stirring. Add onions and celery. Cook until onions are clear. Add garlic, parsley, salt, cayenne pepper, and paprika. Add liquid from oysters and stir well. Add water; cook for 5 minutes. Add oysters. Cook until oysters curl. Remove tops from shells and set aside. Divide oysters and liquid evenly into the patty shells. Place tops over filled patties. Heat in 375-degree oven for 10 minutes. Serve hot. Yield: 6 patties.

DEEP-FRIED OYSTERS

12 nice plump salty oysters
3 cups vegetable oil
1 tsp. black pepper
2 cups corn flour

Drain liquid from oysters. Heat oil in heavy skillet. Mix pepper in corn flour. If oysters are not salty, add ½ teaspoon salt to corn flour. Shake oysters in corn flour. Drop oysters in hot oil and fry for 7 to 10 minutes or until golden. Be careful not to overfry.

Meats

Rock Teacher by Winston Falgout

Getting used to eating so much meat in New Orleans was hard for me at first. The city is different from the country, because in the country the vegetable was the main course and the meat was the accompaniment. In the country, Mother would get up and cook this big pot of greens and put pork chops on the side.

These days, if you told your children that you were having string beans for dinner, they would think you were crazy. You had better tell them you are having some meat first. Not in the country, though—there the vegetable was it.

When we did have meat, it was usually veal. We would go to the butcher to buy it. He always had to cut it before your very eyes—nobody would dream of taking meat that had already been cut!

We raised hogs, and when it was time for a slaughter, all the relatives would come. The men did the butchering and then the women cooked the meat. But these things are of course simpler now. In this section you will find some tasty recipes for all kinds of meat cuts.

BAKED HAM

8- to 10-lb. boneless
    cooked ham
1 cup dark brown sugar
½ cup yellow mustard
1 tsp. ground cloves
2 cups pineapple juice
1 8-oz. bottle of cola
1 can cherry pie filling
Pineapple slices
Maraschino cherries

Remove all wrappings from ham—any strings or paper also. Stick ham several times with metal skewer or long fork. This is to let sauce penetrate ham. Place ham in deep roasting pan.

Mix sugar, mustard, and cloves together. Rub over entire ham. Pour juice and cola in pan around ham. Place in oven and bake for 35 minutes at 350 degrees. Baste ham with juice. With a pastry brush, brush pie filling over ham. Let cook for 10 minutes. Repeat the basting until all pie filling is used. Raise oven temperature to 375 degrees and let glaze cook well. Garnish baked ham with pineapple slices and Maraschino cherries. Yield: 12 servings.

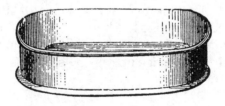

CREOLE JAMBALAYA

1 lb. smoked ham (cubed)
½ lb. chaurice (hot
   sausage cut in pieces)
½ lb. smoked sausage
   (cut in ½-inch slices)
1 cup chopped onions
3 cups uncooked rice
¼ cup chopped green
   onions
½ tsp. paprika
1 tbsp. chopped parsley
1 tsp. ground thyme
1 tsp. chopped garlic
½ cup chopped green
   pepper
1 tsp. salt
1 bay leaf
1 lb. shrimp (peeled and
   deveined)
4 cups boiling water

Place ham, sausages, and onions in 3-quart saucepan. Cover and cook over medium heat until onions are soft. No need to add any oil as the meat will provide enough fat for cooking. Add rice and stir well. Add all other ingredients. Bring to a boil. Let boil for 5 minutes. Lower heat. Cover pot tightly and let cook slowly for 35 minutes or until rice is tender. With a fork, fluff rice up, mixing sausages well. Yield: 6 to 8 servings.

PORK AND RICE CASSEROLE

2 tbsp. olive oil
1 lb. cubed pork
2 tbsp. chopped celery
½ cup chopped green
    onions
2 cups rice
1 tsp. curry powder
1 tbsp. chopped parsley
1 tsp. salt
¼ tsp. cayenne pepper
¼ cup raisins
4 cups water
¼ cup chopped pecans
1 whole ripe tomato (cut in
    eighths)

Put olive oil in frying pan. Add cubed pork and cook for 15 minutes, turning pork often. Add celery and green onions and cook for 5 minutes. Stir rice in pork mixture. Add curry, parsley, salt, cayenne pepper, and raisins. Turn mixture into deep casserole and add water. Cover dish tightly. Place in 350-degree oven and cook 35 to 40 minutes.

Check rice for tenderness. Stir rice at this time. Add pecans and tomato wedges. Cover again and continue to bake for 10 minutes. Yield: 4 to 6 servings.

BUSHALINI

This is really my sister Eleanor's recipe and the name she gave it. I've checked any number of Italian cookbooks and asked some people with Italian backgrounds about this so-called "Bushalini," but all in vain. No one has ever heard of such a dish. This had to be a figment of my sister's own imagination.

Eleanor's husband and six wonderful children would be the first to tell you her cooking is nothing to shout about. But whatever this recipe is, it's a tasty one.

1 lb. elbow macaroni
4 tbsp. olive oil
½ lb. Italian sausage (cut in pieces)
1 lb. smoked ham (cubed)
2 tbsp. flour
½ cup chopped onions
½ cup chopped green peppers
1 tsp. chopped garlic
2 tbsp. tomato paste
1 cup whole tomatoes
2 cups water
1 tsp. oregano
½ tsp. black pepper
½ tsp. cayenne pepper
1 tbsp. chopped parsley
½ cup chopped green onions
1 tsp. salt
½ cup sliced mushrooms
¼ cup grated Romano cheese

Boil macaroni until just tender. Drain and set aside. In deep saucepan heat 2 tablespoons of the olive oil. Sauté sausages and ham for at least 5 to 6 minutes. Remove from pot and set aside. Heat the other 2 tablespoons of olive oil and brown flour in it, stirring constantly (it need not be too brown). Add onions; stir and cook until clear. Add green peppers and garlic. Stir in tomato paste; stir well, being careful not to let paste stick. Add whole tomatoes, including liquid. Add water, oregano, black pepper, cayenne pepper, parsley, green onions, and salt. Stir well.

Return meat to sauce. Let simmer for 15 minutes. Add mushrooms; cook for another 5 minutes. Place macaroni in baking dish. Pour over sauce, tossing lightly. Sprinkle with Romano cheese. Bake in 375-degree oven for 10 minutes. Yield: 6 servings.

BOILED SPARERIBS
WITH SWEET POTATOES

4 lb. pickled spareribs
Water to cover
3 large sweet potatoes
  (peeled and quartered)
¼ cup sugar
½ tsp. ground cinnamon

Cut ribs apart, place in Magnalite stockpot, and cover with water. Slowly boil ribs until tender, about 45 minutes. Add sweet potatoes. Let simmer until potatoes are tender. Be careful not to let potatoes break. When all is done remove to serving platter. Arrange sweet potatoes around meat. Mix sugar and cinnamon and sprinkle over potatoes. Yield: 4 servings.

TUTTI FRUTTI PORK

**1 boneless pork loin
  (about 5 lb.)**
Salt and pepper
**½ cup chopped dried
  apricot**
6 seedless prunes (chopped)
**½ cup finely chopped
  candied pineapple**
**¼ cup finely chopped
  candied red cherries**
¾ cup apricot nectar
½ cup Madeira wine

If pork loin is not split you will have to split it down the side. Salt and pepper meat well.

Mix chopped fruit together. Add 1 tablespoon of apricot nectar. Mix well, then fill loin with fruit mixture. With a good cotton string, tie roast to keep mixture in loin. Place in shallow baking pan. Pour remaining apricot nectar and the Madeira wine over meat. Bake at 365 degrees for 35 to 40 minutes. Baste roast with juices from time to time. When roast is cooked, remove string and slice loin. Yield: 6 to 8 servings.

LEAH'S STUFFED PORK CHOPS

3 slices stale bread
1 pt. oysters in liquid
¼ cup water
½ cup vegetable oil
1 large onion (chopped)
½ cup chopped celery
1 tbsp. chopped garlic
2 tbsp. chopped parsley
1 tsp. salt
¼ tsp. ground thyme
½ tsp. paprika
4 center-cut pork chops,
   1 inch thick (ask butcher
   to cut a pocket in each
   chop)
Salt and pepper for pork
⅓ cup water

Preheat oven at 350 degrees. Break bread into pieces in a bowl. Drain the oyster liquid over the bread and add the ¼ cup of water. Let the bread soak until soft. In a skillet put oil, onions, and celery and cook until clear. Add soaked bread and continue to cook.

Chop oysters and add to mixture. Add garlic, parsley, the teaspoon of salt, the thyme, and the paprika; cook for 20 minutes over medium heat. Let mixture cool. Season pork chops inside and out with salt and pepper. Stuff pork chops with dressing. Secure pork chops with small skewers or heavy toothpicks. Place pork chops in a baking pan. Add the ⅓ cup of water and cover tightly with foil. Bake for 35 minutes. Baste pork chops and bake 10 more minutes. Uncover pan and let brown. Yield: 4 servings.

PORK CHOPS
WITH SAUTEED ONIONS

We were very poor growing up. We didn't have big cabinets. My daddy built shelves underneath the house with a little door and that was where we stored the jellies and jams. I have nephews who still remember when we had to crawl under the house for those. It was under the cool side of the house. There were canned pears and other fruits too. And in those days, when hog-killing time came you knew you were going to have a lot of pork. We left it in the lard and cooked it later right in the lard. The lard preserved the meat, down under the house. I learned later that this process had a fancy name: *confit*.

> **2 tsp. salt**
> **2 tsp. black pepper**
> **4 center-cut pork chops**
> **2 tbsp. flour**
> **¼ cup margarine**
> **½ cup water**
> **2 large onions (sliced)**
> **Chopped parsley**

Mix 1 teaspoon of the salt and 1 teaspoon of the black pepper. Sprinkle salt mixture over both sides of pork chops. Pat flour over chops. In a Magnalite fryer, heat margarine. Brown chops on both sides. Remove chops from fryer. Deglaze pot with water, stirring up all residue. Return chops to fryer. Add sliced onions and remaining salt and pepper. Lower heat. Cover pot tightly. Cook slowly for 10 minutes. Sprinkle with parsley. Yield: 4 servings.

PORK CHOPS
WITH SMOTHERED TURNIPS

4 center-cut pork chops
2 tsp. salt
1 tsp. black pepper
⅓ cup vegetable oil
4 lb. turnips (peeled and
    cubed)
½ cup chopped onions
1 tsp. chopped garlic
2 tbsp. chopped green
    onions
1 tbsp. chopped parsley
½ tsp. ground thyme
½ tsp. cayenne pepper

Season pork chops with 1 teaspoon of the salt and the black pepper. Heat oil and cook pork chops in hot oil for 5 minutes, turning to brown each side. Remove from pot and set aside. Add turnips and onions to pot; cover and cook for 10 minutes. Turnips should begin to get soft. Uncover pot and stir, adding garlic, remaining salt, green onions, parsley, thyme, and cayenne pepper. Stir well. Add pork chops. Lower heat and let cook until turnips are tender, about 30 to 40 minutes. Yield: 4 servings.

STEWED TRIPE
WITH PIGS' FEET

An attorney came to me once and said he was having a party at his house. He wanted something different with these unusual country dishes. My mother made tripe all the time when I was growing up. She would boil it real good and put it in a batter and bread it. The best thing in the world is young tripe breaded. She used to do tripe stew too.

This man also wanted pigs' feet. Cooked pigs' feet really are one of the best things in the world. When you grind the skin and the meat, it makes a strange kind of mixture. It is very fluffy. My mother used to pick the pigs' feet off and grind them to make hogs' head cheese, but people didn't really eat pigs' feet in the Creole homes. For the attorney's sake, though, I worked up this recipe for stewed tripe and pigs' feet.

I did stewed pigs' feet on the lunch menu at the restaurant once. There was one lady who was so happy to get that. She was from North Carolina and said that she hadn't had that in such a long time. It is times like that when doing something different and exciting is rewarding.

2 lb. tripe (cleaned)
4 pigs' feet (split)
2 bay leaves
½ tsp. crushed red pepper
3 sprigs fresh thyme or
   1 tsp. dried thyme leaves
2 tsp. salt
1 tbsp. vegetable oil
2 tbsp. flour
2 onions (chopped)
1 green pepper (chopped)
½ cup chopped celery
3 cups whole tomatoes
¼ tsp. cayenne pepper

Scrape pigs' feet well. Wash tripe and pigs' feet in cold water. Cut tripe in squares about 1 inch thick. Place tripe and pigs' feet in large pot. Cover with hot water. Add bay leaves, crushed red pepper, thyme, and 1 teaspoon of the salt. Bring to a hard boil. Lower heat and let simmer for 2 hours. Remove from water. Let drain. Save 3 cups of stock.

In heavy pot heat oil. Add flour, stirring and watching until barely brown. Add onions; stir. Cook until onions are clear. Add green pepper and celery. Add tomatoes and 3 cups of stock. Stir well. Add remaining salt and cayenne pepper. Cut split pigs' feet in half; remove and discard toes.

Place tripe and pigs' feet in tomato sauce. Cover and let simmer for 45 minutes on a slow heat. Tripe and pigs' feet should be tender. Serve over rice. Yield: 6 servings.

LEG OF LAMB WITH OKRA

1 4- to 5-lb. lamb leg
  (shank part removed)
1 tbsp. salt
1 tbsp. black pepper
1 tbsp. curry powder
6 cloves garlic
½ cup flour
½ cup vegetable oil
1 cup water
8 to 10 small okra

Wash lamb and pat dry with paper towels. Mix salt, pepper, and curry powder together. Make six slits about an inch long and an inch deep into lamb. Fill each slit with 1 clove garlic and salt mixture. Rub extra salt mixture over outside of lamb. Pat flour over lamb.

Put oil and water in roasting pan. Place lamb in pan. Cook in 350-degree oven, basting from time to time, for about 45 minutes to 1 hour. Drop okra around lamb and cook for another 15 to 20 minutes. Okra should not cook too long. Serve with parsley buttered rice. Yield: 6 to 8 servings.

CREOLE MEATBALLS

2 lbs. ground beef
½ cup chopped onions
3 cloves garlic (finely
chopped)
1 tbsp. parsley
1 egg (beaten)
¼ cup Pet milk
1½ tsp. salt
2 tsp. black pepper
½ cup seasoned bread
crumbs
½ cup flour

Place ground beef in mixing bowl. Add all ingredients except flour and mix well. Shape into balls. Should make 8 meatballs. Dust meatballs with flour and place on a greased baking pan. Place in 350-degree oven and bake until brown. Add to gravy.

GRAVY
½ cup vegetable oil
2 tbsp. flour
½ cup chopped onions
¼ cup chopped green
peppers
1 cup whole tomatoes
1 bay leaf
½ tsp. oregano leaves
½ tsp. salt
1 tsp. black pepper
1½ cups water

In a heavy saucepot, heat vegetable oil. Add flour to hot oil and brown flour, stirring constantly. Add onions; stir and cook until tender. Add green peppers, whole tomatoes, bay leaf, oregano, salt, and pepper. Stir in water. Let simmer for about 10 minutes. Add meatballs to gravy. Continue to cook for another 10 minutes. Unlike Italian meatballs, Creoles served these over rice instead of spaghetti. Yield: 8 meatballs.

BURGER STEAK
—CREOLE STYLE

2 lb. ground chuck
1/4 cup finely chopped
   green peppers
1 tbsp. salt
1 tbsp. black pepper
½ tsp. ground thyme
1 egg (beaten)
¼ cup Pet milk
1 clove garlic (finely
   chopped)
¼ cup plain bread crumbs
1 tbsp. parsley (chopped)
2 tbsp. margarine
2 medium onions (sliced)
1 tsp. Tabasco sauce
1 large ripe tomato (cut in
   eighths)

Mix ground chuck with green peppers, salt, pepper, thyme, egg, milk, garlic, bread crumbs, and parsley. Mix well. Divide meat mixture in four parts. Flatten each out into an inch-thick steak. Place margarine in large skillet over medium heat. Place steaks in hot pan; brown on each side. Place sliced onions over steaks. Sprinkle with Tabasco sauce. Cover and let simmer until onions are clear but not too soft. Add tomatoes. Cook about 3 minutes longer. Yield: 4 hamburger steaks.

BOILED BEEF BRISKET
WITH MUSTARD SAUCE

2 lb. boneless beef brisket
Water to cover
1 medium onion (peeled)
1 large carrot (sliced)
1 cup sliced celery
1 whole red pepper
1 tsp. salt

Place brisket in large pot and cover with water. Add onions, carrots, celery, red pepper, and salt. Bring to a boil. Lower heat. Let boil for 1 hour until beef is tender. Remove from pot, reserving vegetables and liquid for sauce. Set brisket aside and cover. Prepare Mustard Sauce below, and serve sauce with the boiled beef. Yield: 4 servings.

MUSTARD SAUCE
Vegetables from brisket
½ cup liquid from brisket
1 cup mayonnaise
½ cup Creole mustard

Take all vegetables that have boiled with brisket and place in blender with ½ cup of liquid. Blend until smooth. To mixture add mayonnaise and Creole mustard. Blend well.

BEEF A LA MODE

½ lb. bacon
5 lb. boneless round steak
2 tbsp. ground cloves
1 tbsp. salt
1 tbsp. black pepper
2 tbsp. flour
¼ cup vegetable oil
2 cups water
½ cup celery (cut in ½-inch
　pieces)
1 whole onion (chopped)
1 cup cubed white potatoes
2 whole carrots (scraped
　and cut in thirds)
1 cup cut green beans

Cut bacon in 1-inch pieces. Make slits in roast. Stuff each slit with bacon and pinch of cloves, using all of the ground cloves.

Mix salt and pepper. Rub entire roast with mixture. Dust roast with flour.

In a small Magnalite roaster, heat oil. Place roast in hot oil; brown on all sides. Add 1 cup of the water. Let simmer on medium heat for 45 minutes, turning from time to time. Add celery, onions, potatoes, carrots, and green beans. Add remaining water. Cook for 20 minutes until all vegetables are tender. Yield: 6 to 8 servings.

POCKET ROAST

6 slices stale bread
1 cup water
48 oysters in liquid
¼ cup vegetable oil
½ lb. ground chuck
2 cups chopped onions
1 cup chopped celery
1 tbsp. chopped garlic
2 tbsp. chopped parsley
1 tsp. ground thyme
2 tbsp. salt
1 tsp. cayenne pepper
1 tbsp. black pepper
3 whole cloves garlic
10 lb. pocket roast
  (shoulder roast with bone
  removed)
¼ cup flour

Place stale bread in bowl. Pour water and oyster liquid over bread. Let soak until bread is very soft.

In heavy pot heat oil. Add the ground chuck, onions, celery, chopped garlic, parsley, and thyme. Mix well, breaking meat up as you stir. Squeeze all liquid from bread. Add bread to meat mixture, pouring in oysters, 1 teaspoon of the salt, and the cayenne pepper. Mix well. Let cook for 30 minutes over medium heat until all seasonings and meat are done. Remove from heat; let cool just enough to handle.

Mix remaining salt with black pepper. Cut cloves of garlic in half. With small knife, make ½-inch slits in thick part of roast and stuff with garlic and salt and pepper mixture. Open roast. Fill opening with oyster stuffing. Do not pack too tight.

Close opening with skewers or tie with cord to hold stuffing. Pat flour over roast. Put roast in pan. Cover and place in 350-degree oven for 1 hour. Remove cover. Baste roast and cook for another 30 to 40 minutes until done and a little brown. Roast will cut better if allowed to cool a little. Yield: 12 to 14 servings.

BEEF DAUBE

1 4-lb. chuck roast
4 cloves garlic
Salt and pepper
Flour
½ cup bacon drippings
2 cups water
1 large carrot (sliced)
3 cups whole tomatoes
1 green pepper (chopped)
1 medium onion (chopped)
¼ cup chopped green
  onions
1 tbsp. chopped parsley

Make four slits in roast. Stuff each slit with garlic, salt, and pepper. Rub outside of roast with salt and pepper. Pat flour over entire roast. Heat bacon drippings in Magnalite Dutch oven. Place roast in pot and brown on all sides. Add water and carrots. Cover and cook over medium heat for 45 minutes. Remove cover. Add tomatoes and all other ingredients. Salt and pepper to taste. Continue to cook for 15 or 20 minutes. Meat should be nice and tender. Excellent over rice or spaghetti. Yield: 6 servings.

BEEF TONGUE
IN BROWN GRAVY

1 fresh beef tongue
Water to cover
3 cloves garlic
1 tsp. salt
1 tsp. black pepper
¼ cup vegetable oil
2 tbsp. flour
1 medium onion (chopped)
2 cups water
1 tbsp. chopped parsley

Wash tongue well. Place tongue in large pot. Cover with water. Boil for about 1 hour. Remove tongue from water. Remove all skin from tongue. Trim tip and back of tongue. Make slits in tongue and stuff with garlic, salt, and pepper.

Heat oil in a Magnalite Dutch oven. Dust tongue with flour, covering all sides. Place tongue in hot oil. Brown on all sides. Lower heat. Add onion and the 2 cups of water. Cover tightly and let simmer on medium heat for about 45 minutes. Sprinkle with parsley. Slice and serve with rice. Yield: 4 servings.

BREADED CALF'S LIVER
WITH BACON

2 eggs (well beaten)
1 cup Pet milk
1 tsp. salt
1 tsp. black pepper
1 lb. calf's liver (sliced ¼
    inch thick)
½ lb. bacon
½ cup Italian bread crumbs

Mix eggs and milk; beat in salt and pepper. Pour over liver and let soak for about 10 minutes. Heat skillet; lay bacon strips in hot skillet. Brown bacon and remove. Lay out on paper on towels. Lower heat.

Take liver out of marinade. Pat in bread crumbs, covering well. Brown liver in bacon fat, turning to brown on both sides. Lay on hot platter. Place bacon over liver; serve. Yield: 3 to 4 servings.

BAKED MEAT LOAF

1 lb. ground beef
½ lb. ground pork
1 cup chopped onions
½ cup chopped green
  peppers
½ cup chopped celery
1 tsp. salt
1 tsp. black pepper
2 eggs (beaten)
½ cup Pet milk
½ cup seasoned bread
  crumbs
2 cloves garlic (chopped)
1 tbsp. chopped parsley
Flour

Put ground beef and pork in a bowl. Add all other ingredients except flour. Mix well. Shape into a ball. Place in baking dish and work meat into a loaf shape. Sprinkle meat with flour. Bake at 350 degrees for 40 minutes until meat is brown and tender. Yield: 4 servings.

GRILLADES

We only serve grillades for dinner at the restaurant. On special occasions we will serve them with grits in the morning, but that is not the way the old Creoles at home did it. That is maybe the way Uptown Creoles did it. Grillades were our dinner where I grew up. They were served with rice or jambalaya.

I think the best grillades I ever had were made with veal "seven" steak. Those were common "depression steaks," and were called seven steaks because the bone is a perfect seven if you get into the center of the shoulder where the shoulder blade is.

Most of the time we had vegetables without any meat, but on Sundays, when we got money if Daddy had a job at the Jahncke Shipyard and things were good, we got veal round steaks. Otherwise, we had seven steaks. Mother would bread those steaks and we would get by. It is funny to me that everybody wants the depression steak now. That was always a big treat to us back then too.

Here is my grillades recipe, using round steak.

> **2 medium veal round steaks**
> **Salt and pepper**
> **¼ cup vegetable oil**
> **2 tbsp. flour**
> **1 medium onion (chopped)**
> **¼ cup chopped celery**
> **1 green pepper (chopped)**
> **1 8-oz. can tomato sauce**
> **2 cloves garlic (chopped)**
> **1 tsp. salt**
> **½ tsp. cayenne pepper**
> **3 cups water**
> **1 whole ripe tomato**
> **2 sprigs thyme**
> **2 tbsp. parsley**

Cut rounds into pieces, leaving meat around the bone. Season meat with salt and black pepper. Set aside. In a Magnalite chicken fryer, heat vegetable oil. Add meat and cover pot. Cook over medium heat for 15 minutes. Uncover and remove meat from pot. Set aside.

Add flour to meat drippings, stirring constantly. Cook until flour is brown. Add onions and celery, stirring until onions are just barely soft. Add green pepper, tomato sauce, garlic, the teaspoon of salt, and the cayenne pepper. Stir mixture. Add water. Dip fresh tomato in boiling water; peel off thin outer skin. Cut tomato into six wedges and add to sauce. Add thyme and parsley. Return meat to pot with sauce. Cover and let simmer for 30 minutes. Yield: 4 to 6 servings.

VEAL PANE

This dish, as I remember, was a must for Sunday dinners. It was just called "pané meat." Veal round steaks were always used for this recipe. It was important to have the rounds cut to the right thickness, about a half-inch. Steaks were trimmed and cut into serving-size pieces, always leaving the small round bone intact. When fried, the marrow in this bone is delicious.

The meat was never beaten as one would do to a cutlet. For frying the veal, my mother always used the big cast-iron frying pan (today I use a Magnalite chicken fryer). The veal was carefully fried so as not to burn the breading.

The sight of the large white platters heaped with golden brown meat always brought broad smiles from everyone. It was equally as good when served cold.

Today at Dooky's we serve veal pané with jambalaya, prepared just as it was done at my home.

2 cups bread crumbs
1 tsp. paprika
3 eggs (beaten)
1½ cups Pet milk
2 large veal round steaks
1 tbsp. salt
1 tbsp. black pepper
2 cups vegetable oil

Mix bread crumbs and paprika; set aside. Add beaten eggs to milk and beat together until well blended.

Trim skin and fat from steaks and cut into serving pieces. Do not remove bones. Salt and pepper veal on both sides. Place in milk mixture. Be sure that all sides are well coated. Let sit in mixture for about 10 minutes.

Dredge meat in crumbs. Heat oil in heavy pan. Oil should be just hot enough to start frying meat. Do not turn on high heat. Place meat in hot oil and brown on both sides. Cook until meat is done, about 10 minutes. Yield: 6 servings.

STUFFED BREAST OF VEAL

Meat was served mostly on special occasions because we didn't have the money to buy it when I was coming up in the depression. We would go to the butcher shop and the man would cut the meat. If we had the money, we bought veal. We didn't have anything else in the country. We didn't have all of the inspections on meat that we have today either. Now we can enjoy veal more often. This is a wonderful recipe for it.

1 veal breast
Salt and pepper
½ lb. veal meat trimmed
   from breast bones and
   ground
¼ cup bacon drippings or
   margarine
1 lb. ground smoked ham
1 cup chopped green onions
1 tsp. salt
1 tsp. coarse ground black
   pepper
½ lb. sliced fresh
   mushrooms
½ tsp. thyme leaves
1 tbsp. chopped parsley
1 cup seasoned bread
   crumbs
1 egg (beaten)

Remove bones from veal breast. Remove some of thin layer of skin. With a meat hammer, beat out veal just a little. Salt and pepper; set aside.

Remove other veal meat from bones. Grind these scraps to get the ground meat. (Save bones for future stock or soup.) In a heavy pot, place bacon drippings and add ground veal and ham. Stir well. Add green onions, the teaspoon of salt, and the coarse pepper. Cook while stirring, about 10 minutes.

Add mushrooms and thyme. Cook until all ingredients are done. Add parsley and bread crumbs. Add beaten egg to mixture and place in center of veal. Roll sides and ends over dressing, forming a neat roll. Tie securely with cord. Place in a greased baking pan. Cover with foil and bake for 45 minutes at 350 degrees.

Remove foil. Baste veal with drippings. Cook for another 25 minutes. Veal should be nice and tender. Sliced mushrooms may be added to the gravy. Yield: 6 to 8 servings.

VEAL STEW WITH VEGETABLES

Salt and pepper
2 lb. veal brisket stew meat
1 lb. boneless veal stew
  meat
¼ cup vegetable oil
2 tbsp. flour
½ cup chopped onions
¼ cup chopped celery
1 8-oz. can tomato sauce
1 qt. water
2 medium carrots (scraped
  and cut in 1-inch pieces)
2 medium white potatoes
  (quartered)
1 tbsp. salt
1 tsp. crushed red pepper
1 tsp. chopped garlic
½ cup chopped green
  peppers
½ cup green peas

Salt and pepper meat. In 5-quart saucepan, heat oil over medium heat. Add meat, cover, and let steam for 15 minutes. Turn meat over and cook for another 10 minutes. Remove meat from pot and set aside. In same pot add flour, stirring constantly. Let flour brown just slightly.

Add onions and celery and stir. Cook slowly for 5 minutes. Slowly stir in tomato sauce and water; add meat and simmer for 10 minutes. Add carrots, potatoes, salt, crushed pepper, garlic, and green peppers. Cook for 10 minutes. Add green peas and let cook until all vegetables are tender. Serve over rice. Yield: 6 servings.

Miracle in the Delta by Clifton G. Webb

The Wild Game Dinner is an annual tradition at Dooky Chase's for local politicians. It started in 1978 when Dutch Morial, the mayor of New Orleans at the time, had these ducks in his freezer. His wife, Sybil, said she wanted them out. Sybil is so easygoing, to look at her you wouldn't think she could crack an egg. She doesn't have to get loud. She would say something, and even Dutch would move. So he brought these ducks over to me and figured he would dump them in my lap. We started with forty ducks.

We were about to have the police strike and still, everybody came to the dinner. Even Dutch's worst enemies came. All of the police and people who were getting ready to strike on him were there. He would try to send messages through people but they refused to "tell tales" for him. It go so red hot that I had to leave.

Now, every year the men bring me the game and I cook it the way I please, starting the week before the dinner. No one tells me how to prepare it or what to prepare. Anyone can come to the party, but they have to bring some kind of game. We usually have a feel for how many people are going to be there ahead of time. When there is a lot of political upheaval, this is the "in" spot. I provide the meal and they provide the spice. Yes, they do provide the spice.

Dutch's last year in office was 1986. That year we moved the dinner to the Coker Room in the Municipal Auditorium, because Gallier Hall, where we usually held it, was being renovated. That day Dutch was at his meanest. He was in the worst form you could ever find him in. Everything went well though; we had a lot of people there.

We told Dutch that this was the last time we were going to hold the dinner because he was going out of office. We presented him with a pair of Charlie Hutchinson wood-carved ducks, and made the announcement. The men said, "Oh no, we're not going to end here. We're going to continue this."

So the next year, even with Dutch out of office, it was time to start planning the dinner. We had no idea how many people were going to be there because they were so mad at Dutch when he left office. The invitations went out, and to my surprise, the ducks started coming in like crazy. We ended up serving over 350 people.

I'll never forget one year when somebody had to clean up Audubon Zoo as punishment for illegally shooting some ducks. He went over the bag limit or shot the ducks out of season or something and the game warden caught him. I told Dutch he had to keep his mouth shut and not tell people where he was getting these ducks because you never know who is at the dinner. We laugh about those ducks now. We'll say, "I think this duck came out of City Park. I don't see any bullet holes in this thing."

I have to say, 1988 was the living end. One young man brought these doves, sat in the middle of my kitchen, and started cleaning them. He was a jeweler's son-in-law and came to my place wearing all of this jewelry and gold. He kept saying, "Oh God, I didn't know I was coming across from the projects." I said, "Well, did you see any lions or tigers over there?" He said, "No." I said, "Those black folks stopped eating white folks a long time ago." The next time he came, he had a little gun on his belt. I said, "Man, if those black folks in the projects were really rough, they would make you eat that little gun." Seriously, my customers have never encountered any problems due to the location of the restaurant.

A lot of recipes have developed from these annual Wild Game Dinners. These should help you serve up your game in some delicious ways.

RICE DRESSING

8 chicken gizzards
Water to cover
8 chicken livers
2 tbsp. margarine
½ lb. ground beef
1 lb. hot pork sausage
1 cup chopped onions
1 tsp. chopped garlic
½ cup chopped celery
¼ cup chopped green
  pepper
1 tbsp. chopped parsley
¼ tsp. ground thyme
1 tsp. salt
½ tsp. crushed red pepper
½ tsp. black pepper
4 cups cooked rice
Seasoned bread crumbs

Place gizzards in pot and add water to cover. Bring to boil and let boil for 10 minutes. Add livers to the pot and continue to boil for another 5 minutes—water should be just about boiled out. Set aside. In a thick pot, melt margarine. Add ground beef and sausage and mix together well. Add onions, garlic, celery, and green pepper. Let cook over medium heat.

Remove livers and gizzards from water. Chop them very fine. Add to meat mixture and continue to cook for 15 to 20 minutes until meat and seasonings are cooked. Add parsley, thyme, salt, crushed red pepper, and black pepper. Stir well. Stir rice into mixture. Mix well. Pour into 2-quart glass baking dish and sprinkle with seasoned bread crumbs. Heat in 350-degree oven for 10 minutes. Excellent with wild game.

PHEASANT
WITH RAISIN SAUCE

2 pheasants
Salt and white pepper
1 whole onion
1 rib celery
6 strips bacon

Rub pheasants with clean towel inside and out. Mix salt and white pepper. Rub birds inside and out with salt and pepper mixture. Cut onion in half. Fill cavity of each bird with ½ onion and piece of celery.

Cover each bird with 3 strips of bacon. Place in shallow baking pan. Cover with foil. Place in 350-degree oven. Bake for 45 minutes. Remove foil and bake for 15 minutes or until birds are tender. Pour Raisin Sauce over pheasants. Yield: 4 to 6 servings.

RAISIN SAUCE
3 tbsp. butter
3 tbsp. drippings from
  baked pheasants
3 tbsp. flour
½ cup chopped green
  onions
¼ cup chopped celery leaves
1 cup burgundy wine
1 tbsp. brown sugar
1½ cups water
¼ tsp. allspice
1½ cups raisins

Melt butter in saucepot and add drippings. Add flour and cook until light brown. Add green onions and celery leaves. Stir well. Slowly add wine and brown sugar. Continue cooking on medium heat. Add water and allspice. Stir well. Wash raisins and add them to sauce. Bring to a slow boil. Lower heat and simmer for 5 minutes.

WILD DUCKS AND TURNIPS

When the ducks began to get scarce, the men started bringing in anything they would shoot for the Wild Game Dinner. Somebody might have a friend in the next state who would supply ducks. There is one man who brings hogs' head cheese and rabbits. He is proud as peaches of his hogs' head cheese.

One year the bag limit was three ducks. What are you going to do with three ducks? We ended up with only thirty or forty wild ducks that year, but everybody wanted to come to the dinner. One man sent three cases of domestic ducks. Another got cases of Cornish hens. There were rabbits and deer—I think I prepared five whole deer in 1988. It never stops. Ducks have been the tradition at the dinners, though, and this how I prepare them.

> **2 wild ducks**
> **2 tbsp. chopped garlic**
> **Salt and black pepper**
> **¼ cup flour**
> **½ tsp. paprika**
> **¼ tsp. garlic powder**
> **6 strips bacon**
> **3 cups water**
> **1 cup chopped onion**
> **2 sprigs fresh thyme**
> **2 large turnips (diced)**
> **½ tsp. white pepper**
> **1 tbsp. chopped parsley**

Ducks should be picked well; no feathers should be left on the birds. Pass birds over an open flame on stove; this will singe small feathers. Hold birds under running water, rubbing them briskly to remove all small feathers. Wipe ducks dry. Raise the skin on breast of ducks; rub 1 tablespoon of the chopped garlic under duck skin. Mix salt and pepper. Season ducks by rubbing mixture in cavity of ducks and over the entire birds.

Mix flour, paprika, and garlic powder. Dredge the ducks in the flour mixture. Set birds aside.

Cut bacon in small pieces. In a small Magnalite roaster or Dutch oven, cook bacon pieces until the fat is rendered. Remove cooked bacon from pot. Place prepared ducks in pot, breast side up. Brown ducks on all sides. Add water, onions, remaining garlic, and thyme. Cover tightly and let simmer for 1 hour, turning as ducks cook. When ducks are tender, pour turnips around ducks. Add white pepper, parsley, and bacon pieces. Cover pot and let simmer until turnips are done—about 20 minutes. Yield: 4 servings.

BRAISED QUAIL
WITH CRAB APPLE JELLY

4 quail
Salt and pepper
2 tbsp. butter
1 tbsp. vegetable oil
1 cup water
4 tbsp. crab apple jelly

Split quail down the back; spread open and flatten each bird out. Season with salt and pepper.

Heat butter and oil in skillet. Place birds in hot oil. Brown birds on both sides. When birds are browned, add water. Cover pan and let simmer for 20 minutes. Uncover and brush jelly over quail. Cook slowly, basting quail. Let cook for 5 minutes. Place quail on platter with breast side up; pour drippings over quail. Yield: 4 servings.

QUAIL WITH HAM
AND EGGPLANT DRESSING

4 whole quail
1 large eggplant
¼ cup margarine
1 medium onion (chopped)
1 tsp. chopped parsley
½ lb. ground ham
1 clove garlic (chopped)
Salt and pepper to taste
1 cup seasoned bread
  crumbs

Take cleaned quail and wash and pat dry. Place in bowl and cover with water; set aside.

Peel eggplant and cut into cubes. Place in bowl and cover with water; set aside.

Melt margarine in pot. Add onions; sauté for about 3 or 4 minutes. Add parsley, ham, garlic, salt, and pepper. Drain water off eggplant and add to ham mixture. Cook until eggplant is tender—about 15 minutes. Let cool; mix in bread crumbs. Fill each quail with eggplant dressing. Place quail on greased pan. Bake in 350-degree oven for 45 minutes. Yield: 4 servings.

POULE D'EAU GUMBO

6 poule d'eau (cleaned and
  skinned)
2 cups milk
½ cup vegetable oil
1 lb. smoked ham (cut in
  cubes)
3 tbsp. flour
2 cups chopped onions
1 cup chopped celery
½ cup green onions
1 tsp. chopped garlic
2 qt. water
2 level tbsp. salt
1 tsp. crushed red pepper
½ tsp. cayenne pepper
1 tbsp. chopped parsley
3 sprigs fresh thyme
2 bay leaves
1 tbsp. paprika

Cut birds in quarters. Wash well and put in bowl. Pour milk over birds; let them soak overnight in the refrigerator.

In a 5-quart Magnalite stockpot, heat the oil. Remove birds from milk; rinse them off. Put birds in hot oil and brown on all sides. Add ham; cook for 5 minutes. Remove birds and ham from pot. Set aside.

Add flour to drippings. Brown flour until golden brown. Add onions and celery; cook 5 minutes until onions are clear. Add green onions and garlic. Stir well. Slowly add water, stirring as you pour. Add salt, crushed red pepper, cayenne, parsley, thyme, bay leaves, and paprika. Return ham and poule d'eau to liquid. Let come to a boil. Lower heat and simmer for 45 minutes. Serve over rice. Yield: 6 to 8 servings.

WILD GOOSE WITH APRICOT
AND RICE DRESSING

1 wild goose (around 4 lb.)
Salt and black pepper
1 tbsp. butter
½ cup chopped green
  onions
¼ cup chopped pecans
1 tbsp. chopped celery
  leaves
½ cup chopped dried
  apricots
3 cups converted rice
1 tsp. salt
¼ tsp. crushed red pepper
2 cups apricot nectar
4 cups water
1 whole onion (chopped)

Make sure the hunter who gets the goose cleans the bird thoroughly. Wash bird inside and out, clearing cavity well. Season well with salt and pepper. Set aside.

In 5-quart pot melt butter; add green onions, pecans, celery leaves, and apricots. Cook for about 4 to 5 minutes over medium heat, stirring occasionally. Add rice, the teaspoon of salt, and the crushed red pepper. Stir well; add 1 cup of the apricot nectar and 3 cups of the water. Stir all ingredients well. Cover pot tightly with aluminum foil, let cook over low heat for 30 minutes until rice is done. Stir rice with fork to mix all ingredients. Remove from heat and let rice cool enough to handle.

Open cavity and push dressing inside goose. Don't pack too tightly—allow a little room for cooking. Secure opening with wooden or metal skewers. (If there is any extra dressing, put it aside and use as garnish for finished goose.)

Place bird in greased baking pan. Place chopped onion around bird with the remaining water. Place bird in preheated 350-degree oven. Bake for 1 hour. Pull out; baste with the remaining apricot nectar. Cook for another 35 minutes or until goose is tender. Yield: 6 servings.

SQUIRREL STEW

2 squirrel (cut up)
2 tsp. salt
2 tsp. black pepper
¼ cup vegetable oil
2 tbsp. flour
1 cup chopped onions
¼ cup chopped green
peppers
2 cloves garlic (chopped)
½ cup burgundy
3 cups water
½ tsp. cayenne pepper
2 bay leaves
1 sprig fresh thyme
1 tbsp. chopped parsley

Cut squirrel in parts. One should make about six pieces. Wash squirrel and rub with 1 teaspoon of the salt and 1 teaspoon of the black pepper. Set aside.

In heavy pan (a Magnalite Dutch oven is excellent) heat the oil. Place squirrel in hot oil, browning on all sides. Lower heat and cover; let steam for 15 minutes. Remove squirrel from pot and set aside. To drippings, add flour. Stir and brown. Add onions and cook for 5 minutes; add green peppers and garlic. Stir; cook for 5 minutes more. Add burgundy, water, the remaining salt, the cayenne pepper, the remaining black pepper, the bay leaves, the thyme, and the parsley; stir well. Return squirrel to gravy; cover pot.

Let cook over medium heat for 35 to 40 minutes. Squirrel should be tender. Serve over rice. Yield: 6 servings.

SQUIRREL PIE

One year my brother brought a lot of squirrels for the Wild Game Dinner. We did squirrel pies, which can be an awful job to do. You have to steam the squirrel until it is tender, pick it all off the bone, and then you make your sauce and put it in a spicy crust. If I don't have enough squirrels to do pies, I have found they make good "critter gumbo" when combined with venison sausage. Squirrel pie, though, is worth the effort.

2 large squirrel
3 cups water
¼ cup vegetable oil
1 tbsp. flour
½ cup chopped onions
½ cup chopped celery
1 clove garlic
1 tbsp. chopped parsley
1 tsp. salt
1 tsp. crushed red pepper
1 tsp. black pepper
1 tbsp. filé powder

Cut squirrel in pieces. Put squirrel to steam in pot with the water. Slowly cook for 45 minutes until tender. Remove from pot and reserve liquid. Let squirrel cool. Pick all meat from bones and set aside.

In skillet heat oil; add flour and lightly brown; add onions and celery. Cook until onions are clear; add garlic, parsley, salt, crushed red pepper, black pepper, and filé powder. Add meat to mixture along with stock that was reserved. Cook for 5 minutes.

Put mixture in pie shell (see below); cover with extra dough; pinch edges of pie. Make ½-inch slit in middle of pie. Bake in 350-degree oven for 30 to 40 minutes. Yield: 4 to 6 servings.

PIE CRUST
2 cups flour
1 tsp. salt
¼ tsp. cayenne pepper
¼ tsp. garlic powder
1 cup shortening
¼ cup water

Place flour in mixing bowl; add all dry ingredients. Mix well. Cut in shortening until flour becomes crumbly and has taken in all of shortening. Add water and mix well. Divide into 2 balls. Let sit in refrigerator for 15 minutes. Roll 1 ball on flat floured surface to fit a 9-inch pie pan. Roll out second ball of dough to fit the top of the pie.

ROAST VENISON
WITH JUNIPER BERRIES

If ever you don't have a recipe to cook something, remember that's not important. You start creating. I have to change menus at the Wild Game Dinners all the time. Once a judge brought in a deer roast for me to work with (the very morning of the dinner!). I cooked the roast with juniper berries. Whatever they give me, I make something out of.

4 to 5 lb. venison roast
2 tbsp. salt
1 tbsp. black pepper
6 strips bacon
1 tbsp. crushed red pepper
5 cloves garlic (chopped)
2 cups water
1 large onion (chopped)
2 tbsp. juniper berries

The night before cooking, wash venison in cold water. With a sharp knife make about six ½-inch-deep slits in roast. Mix salt and black pepper; set aside. Take 2 slices of bacon and cut into small pieces. Hold slits open; push bacon pieces, pinch of salt and pepper mixture, pinch of crushed red pepper, and pinch of garlic into each slit. Rub entire roast with remaining salt and pepper. Cover top of roast with remaining strips of bacon. Put roast in refrigerator and let sit overnight.

Get out a Magnalite Dutch oven and put the water in pot. Place seasoned roast in pot; add chopped onion and juniper berries. Cover tightly and simmer for 1 hour, basting from time to time. Cook until roast is tender. Yield: 8 servings.

VENISON STEAK
WITH RED CABBAGE

1 tbsp. juniper berries
¼ tsp. cayenne pepper
½ tsp. salt
¼ tsp. granulated garlic
¼ cup red wine vinegar
¼ cup vegetable oil
2 small venison steaks or
   4 nice venison chops
4 strips bacon
1 very small red cabbage
Salt for cabbage

Place juniper berries in a cloth and pound them to make a powder. In bowl mix juniper berries, cayenne pepper, salt, granulated garlic, red wine vinegar, and oil. Beat well. Place venison in mixture, tossing well. Cover and let marinate 6 to 8 hours.

In a Magnalite chicken fryer, cook bacon strips until done. Remove bacon and set aside. Place steaks in hot bacon drippings; cook slowly, turning twice. Add all of marinade oils to steaks, cover tightly, and let steaks simmer until tender (about 20 minutes).

Cut cabbage in four parts. Let water run through cabbage—do not separate leaves. Place cabbage around steaks. Crumble bacon over cabbage. Sprinkle salt over cabbage. Cover and cook for 15 minutes or until cabbage is tender. Yield: 4 servings.

RABBIT STEW
—HUNTER'S STYLE

1 rabbit
1 tsp. chopped garlic
Salt and black pepper
½ cup flour
½ cup bacon drippings or
 vegetable oil
½ cup chopped onions
¼ cup chopped celery
¼ cup chopped green
 peppers
1 cup whole tomatoes
1 tsp. whole thyme leaves
1 whole red pepper
¼ tsp. crushed red pepper
2 cups water

Cut rabbit into six pieces. With sharp knife make two small but deep slits in each piece of rabbit. Stuff these openings with garlic and mixture of salt and pepper. Rub pieces with more salt and pepper. Dredge rabbit in flour, coating well.

In heavy Dutch oven, heat bacon drippings (or vegetable oil). Place rabbit in hot oil; brown on all sides. Lower heat and pour onions, celery, and green peppers over rabbit. Cover and simmer for 15 minutes. Stir and add tomatoes, salt, thyme, whole red pepper, crushed red pepper, and water. Toss all ingredients well; cover and cook over medium heat for 30 minutes until rabbit is tender. Serve over rice. Yield: 6 servings.

PANEED RABBIT
WITH VEGETABLES

1 young rabbit
1 tsp. salt
½ tsp. black pepper
¼ cup water
1 large carrot (scraped and
    cut in ½-inch pieces)
1 whole turnip (peeled and
    cubed)
1 onion (quartered)
1 cup Pet milk
2 eggs (beaten)
1 cup vegetable oil
1 cup seasoned bread
    crumbs
1 green pepper (cut in wide
    strips)
Chopped parsley for garnish

Cut rabbit in serving-size pieces. Mix salt and pepper and rub over rabbit. Put rabbit in 2-quart saucepot with the water. Add carrot, turnip, and onion. Let steam for 15 minutes. Remove rabbit and let cool. Save vegetable mixture. Mix milk and eggs well. Pour over cooled rabbit, covering all parts. Let sit for 5 minutes.

In a Magnalite chicken fryer, heat oil. Dredge rabbit pieces in bread crumbs, making sure all pieces are well coated. Place in hot oil; cook on medium heat and brown on both sides until golden. Place on platter. Add green pepper to reserved vegetables. Cook for 5 minutes. Place vegetables around rabbit. Garnish with chopped parsley. Yield: 4 servings.

Poultry

Confrontation at the Bridge by Jacob Lawrence

For a while my father didn't want to raise chickens. They always seemed to get into his precious garden. When the neighbors' chickens would do that, he would hit them with rocks. My mother was worried he would kill one someday.

When my father slowed down a little and reduced the size of his garden, we finally got some chickens. My grandmother had some too. She would kill a chicken for cooking by wringing its neck in one swing. Then she'd put a tub on top of it so it wouldn't flop around. Such chickens were usually isolated in a coop for a time before being killed, so that they could "clean out" or be fattened maybe.

In New Orleans you could go to a place like St. Bernard Market and buy a live chicken. Later on, you could pick one out for them to kill, and then go back to get it. Vendors also went through the city, selling live chickens from their carts.

If my family had a 300-pound hog, we could get 100 pounds of lard out of that. That made the best fried chicken. We would use big iron pots to cook in. That's really not done anymore. My poultry recipes now use oil, but they come out fine!

STEWED TURKEY NECKS

¼ cup vegetable oil
Salt and pepper to taste
2 turkey necks (cut into
   1-inch pieces)
2 tbsp. flour
1 onion (chopped)
½ cup chopped celery
2 cups water
¼ tsp. rosemary leaves
½ tsp. crushed red pepper
½ tsp. paprika
½ tsp. salt

Heat oil in a heavy pot. Salt and pepper necks, place in pot, and cover tightly. Cook over medium heat for 15 minutes. Remove necks from pot and set aside. Cook flour in hot drippings until flour is golden; stir well. Add onions and celery; cook for 5 minutes.

Slowly add water and stir to pick up all the sediment from bottom of pot. Add rosemary, crushed red pepper, paprika, and the ½ teaspoon of salt. Stir well; return turkey necks to gravy. Cover pot and let simmer until necks are tender. Yield: 4 servings.

TURKEY CUTLETS

4 4-oz. turkey cutlets
Salt and white pepper
½ cup Pet milk
¼ cup water
2 eggs (beaten)
1½ cups bread crumbs
1 tbsp. paprika
Vegetable oil for frying

Pound cutlets out. Season to taste with salt and white pepper. Mix milk, water, and beaten eggs. Pour over cutlets, making sure to cover each one. Let sit for several minutes. Mix bread crumbs with paprika. Dredge cutlets in bread crumbs, covering each cutlet on both sides. Fry in hot oil until golden brown. Yield: 4 servings.

TURKEY BEIGNETS

1½ cups self-rising flour
1 tsp. baking powder
1 egg (beaten)
¾ cup milk
2 cups chopped cold turkey
Oil for frying

Sift flour and baking powder. Add egg and milk and mix well. Add turkey to batter. Batter should be thick enough to coat meat. Drop a tablespoon of the batter at a time in hot oil. Turn until beignets are cooked, about 5 minutes. Yield: 8 to 10 beignets.

ROAST TURKEY WINGS

2 turkey wings
Salt and white pepper to
  taste
¼ cup chopped onions
¼ cup chopped celery
1 large carrot (finely
  chopped)
½ cup water
1 tsp. parsley

Cut each wing into four parts. Season with salt and white pepper. Place in shallow baking pan. Sprinkle onions, celery, and carrots over wings. Pour the water in pan. Cover with foil. Bake for 40 minutes in preheated oven at 350 degrees. Take foil from pan, baste wings with sauce, and continue to bake uncovered for 15 minutes until nice and brown. Sprinkle with parsley. Yield: 4 servings.

CHICKEN BREAST STUFFED
WITH OYSTER DRESSING

It wasn't until I changed the whole Dooky Chase's menu to Creole that I really got acceptance from everybody. People got excited when I put stuffed chicken breasts on the menu and went back to veal. The customers really began to feel my presence then. Up till then there had been no integration. The blacks were eating at home and they were happy with their fried foods. But when integration came, it was a whole new ball game because they were able to go all over then. You had to start changing to keep up with the pace. My recipe for Stuffed Chicken Breasts with Oyster Dressing follows.

2 tsp. salt
2 tsp. white pepper
4 7-oz. boneless chicken
    breasts
3 slices stale bread
½ cup water
1 pt. oysters in liquid
½ stick margarine
1 tsp. chopped onions
½ cup chopped celery
¼ tsp. cayenne pepper
1 tsp. chopped garlic
1 tsp. chopped parsley
½ tsp. whole thyme leaves
1 cup sliced mushrooms
1 cup white wine
½ cup chopped onions

Mix 1 teaspoon of the salt with the white pepper. Lay chicken breasts skin side down. Sprinkle with salt and white pepper mixture. Put in refrigerator to chill a little.

Place stale bread in bowl. Pour water over bread. Drain oysters; pour oyster liquid over bread. Let bread soak well.

Heat margarine in saucepot. Add onions and celery; stir. Cook until onions are clear. Squeeze liquid from bread. Add bread to onion mixture. Stir well, breaking up any large pieces of bread. Chop oysters (not too small). Add oysters, cayenne pepper, garlic, parsley, and thyme with the remaining salt. Stir mixture well. Cook for 15 minutes. Let cool. If dressing is too soft, tighten mixture with a little more bread crumbs.

Take chicken from refrigerator; place mound of dressing in the middle of each chicken breast. Fold all sides of breast over stuffing and secure with skewers. Put in pan skewer side up and cover pan with foil. Place in oven and bake at 350 degrees for 40 minutes. Remove foil and turn breasts over so that skin side is up. Let chicken brown a little. Pour mushrooms over chicken. Add wine, stirring well with mushrooms around chicken. Cook for another 10 minutes. Yield: 4 servings.

CHICKEN CLEMENCEAU

3 6-oz. boneless and
   skinless chicken breasts
   (cut in cubes)
Salt and pepper
3 tbsp. butter
½ cup white wine
1 tbsp. chopped garlic
2 cups diced white potatoes
1 cup sliced mushrooms
½ cup cooked green peas
1 tsp. chopped parsley
½ tsp. paprika
White pepper

Season chicken with salt and pepper. In large frying pan, melt butter; add chicken and stir. Let cook for 5 minutes. Add wine, garlic, and potatoes. Cover; let cook for another 5 minutes. Potatoes should be soft and wine just about cooked out.

Uncover and add mushrooms, stirring well. Sauté until mushrooms begin to get soft. Add peas, parsley, and paprika. Cook until well blended, being careful not to mash vegetables. Add salt and white pepper to taste. Yield: 4 servings.

BAKED CHICKEN
IN CARIBBEAN SAUCE

Salt and pepper
1 large frying chicken
   (quartered)

Salt and pepper chicken. Lay chicken skin side up in baking pan. Place in oven at 350 degrees. Bake for 15 minutes.

CARIBBEAN SAUCE
2 tbsp. vegetable oil
1 cup finely chopped onion
1 cup finely chopped celery
¼ cup lime juice
1 cup ketchup
½ cup Pickapepper Sauce
1 cup orange juice
1 oz. rum
1 tsp. crushed red pepper
Parsley and orange slices
   for garnish

To create sauce, place oil in pot and heat a little. Add onions and celery. Stir well. Let cook for 5 minutes, being careful not to burn onions. Add all other sauce ingredients except garnishes, stirring as you add them. Pour over chicken. Let bake about 30 minutes, basting chicken from time to time with sauce. Garnish with parsley and orange slices. Yield: 4 servings.

CHICKEN POIVRE VERT

4 5-oz. chicken breasts
1½ tbsp. green peppercorns
 in water
1 tbsp. salt
1 tbsp. white pepper
1 tbsp. paprika
2 tbsp. butter
½ cup water
2 medium carrots (sliced)
¾ cup fresh or frozen green
 peas
1 large onion (sliced)
½ cup sliced mushrooms
1 large green pepper (sliced)
Parsley

Raise skin on chicken breasts and place peppercorns under skin of each breast. Form breasts into loose rolls. Season chicken with 1 teaspoon of the salt and 1 teaspoon of the white pepper and sprinkle with paprika.

Melt butter in large skillet. Place chicken breasts in hot butter. Brown slightly on all sides. Cook for 5 or 6 minutes. Add water, carrots, and peas; cover and simmer for 10 minutes. Add onion, mushrooms, green pepper, and remaining salt and white pepper. Cook until vegetables are just tender. Vegetables should not cook too much. Sprinkle with parsley. Yield: 4 servings.

CHICKEN CREOLE

**6 5-oz. boneless and
skinless chicken breasts
1 tbsp. salt
½ tsp. white pepper
¼ cup vegetable oil
1 cup chopped onions
½ cup chopped green
peppers
2 cups whole tomatoes
with liquid
2 cups water
2 cloves garlic (mashed and
chopped)
½ tsp. ground thyme (or
2 sprigs fresh)
¼ tsp. cayenne pepper
12 small whole okra
1 lb. shrimp (peeled and
deveined)
1 tbsp. chopped parsley**

Season chicken with 1 teaspoon salt and the white pepper. In large
skillet or chicken fryer, heat the vegetable oil. Place seasoned chicken
in hot oil, turning as it cooks (about 6 minutes). Lower heat. Remove
chicken and set aside.

Sauté onions in skillet until they are clear. Add the green peppers;
stir and cook for 3 or 4 minutes. Add whole tomatoes, mashing them
as you stir them into onion mixture. Add water, garlic, thyme, cayenne
pepper, and remaining salt. Let sauce cook on high heat for 4 minutes.

Lower heat; return chicken to sauce. Add okra and cook for 10
minutes until okra are just tender. Add shrimp; let cook until shrimp
turn pink (about 5 minutes). Add parsley. Serve over buttered rice.
Yield: 6 servings.

CHICKEN CURRY

1 3- to 4-lb. frying chicken
  (cut in 8 parts)
1 tbsp. salt
1 tbsp. white pepper
2 cups flour
¼ cup margarine
1 cup chopped onions
¼ cup chopped celery
½ cup chopped green
  peppers
½ cup chopped green
  onions
1 tsp. chopped garlic
2 cups water
1 tsp. curry powder
2 whole dried red peppers
Pinch of salt
1 tbsp. chopped parsley
1 tbsp. paprika

Pull all fat from chicken. Melt chicken fat in small pot. Sprinkle the tablespoon of salt and the white pepper on all sides of chicken. Shake chicken in flour, coating all pieces well. Pour melted chicken fat plus margarine in a Magnalite chicken fryer and heat. Place chicken parts in hot fat. Brown on all sides; remove chicken and set aside.

Place onions and celery in hot drippings. Stir and let cook for 5 minutes. Add green peppers, green onions, and garlic. Add water, and stir well. Cook for 5 minutes. Add curry powder, red peppers, and a little salt. Return chicken to gravy. Add parsley and paprika. Let simmer for 30 minutes. Yield: 4 servings.

CHICKEN CASSEROLE

1 3-lb. frying chicken
1 tsp. salt
1 carrot
1 onion (cut in half)
1 cup celery (cut in 1-inch
  pieces)
1 whole red pepper
2 qt. water
½ stick margarine
1 tbsp. flour
1 cup evaporated milk
½ lb. fresh mushrooms
  (sliced)
1 tbsp. oregano leaves
1 tbsp. parsley
2 cups artichoke hearts
  (cut in half)
¼ cup bread crumbs
½ tsp. paprika
2 tbsp. grated Romano
  cheese

Cut chicken in half; place in large pot with salt, carrots, onions, celery, and whole red pepper. Pour water over chicken and bring to a boil. Let boil for 20 minutes. Chicken should be tender enough to remove meat from bones.

Remove chicken from water. Let cool. Save the stock. When chicken is cool enough to handle, remove skin (set skin aside) and pull chicken from bones. Discard bones.

Drain vegetables from stock and save at least 2 cups of liquid.

Place vegetables and chicken skin in blender, puree and set aside. In a skillet, heat margarine. Add flour and stir well, cooking for 5 minutes. *Do not brown*.

Stir in the reserved chicken stock and pour in evaporated milk and mushrooms as you stir. Whip until smooth. Add puree, oregano, and parsley. Spread some of the sauce in bottom of a casserole dish. Add layer of chicken and a layer of artichoke. Cover with remaining sauce. Mix crumbs, paprika, and cheese. Sprinkle over top of casserole. Place in 375-degree oven; bake for 25 minutes. Yield: 6 people.

CHICKEN LIVERS
WITH ONIONS AND OYSTERS

1 tsp. salt
1 tsp. black pepper
2 tbsp. flour
24 whole chicken livers
¼ lb. butter
24 oysters (save the liquid)
2 large onions (sliced)
1 tbsp. chopped parsley

Mix ½ teaspoon of the salt and ½ teaspoon of the pepper in flour. Mix well. Dredge livers in seasoned flour. Heat butter in skillet. Brown livers in butter, turning to brown completely. Add oyster liquid; stir livers. Add sliced onions and loosen into rings. Add remaining salt and pepper. Cover. Cook over medium heat for 5 minutes. Onions should be just tender. Add oysters; let simmer until oysters curl. Sprinkle with parsley. May be served with rice or mashed potatoes. Yield: 4 servings.

SOUTHERN FRIED CHICKEN

I remember going to Mardi Gras parades and seeing fried chicken being sold on the street. There really wasn't any Mardi Gras in Madisonville—everybody left for New Orleans in hay trucks. Sometimes I could go, but usually my father wouldn't let us miss school.

We would go to see the Zulu parade, which was on Claiborne Avenue from Canal Street to St. Bernard Avenue. Claiborne was lined with beautiful oaks then. Some of the people held open houses on Claiborne, for their friends. The street was full of booths, with blacks selling fried chicken, fried fish, and red beans. My favorite thing about Mardi Gras was that we could eat in the street. My father never even let us eat candy outside normally.

I also thought it was so fun to dress in costume. But a lot of Creole ladies used the occasion to bring out their first spring suit. They would wear violet corsages, and walk with canes with a celluloid feathered doll on top. I thought it was a shame to get all fancy on Mardi Gras, instead of playing like the other maskers.

The Zulu parade mocked the white parades. The "African King" would wear a huge crystal doorknob as a ring. They were very funny. They wandered all over, passing households that had paid them to go that way. Now Mardi Gras is so big that organized routes need to be followed. That's good to impose some kind of order where so many people are involved.

One group put on a Mardi Gras Breakfast Dance that was very fancy. The invited guests—usually teachers and professionals—would go in hats and gloves. I got invited eventually and wasn't so impressed. I was just happy to be watching the parade, finally able to eat some fried chicken in the street.

1 3-lb. fryer
1 tbsp. salt
1 tbsp. black pepper
2 eggs (beaten)
½ cup Pet milk
½ cup water
2 cups flour
1 tsp. paprika
¼ tsp. ground thyme
½ tsp. granulated garlic
1 qt. oil for frying

Cut chicken in eight pieces. Season well with salt and pepper. Set aside. Mix eggs, milk, and water. Pour mixture over chicken. Let sit for 5 minutes.

In a heavy paper bag, mix flour, paprika, ground thyme, and granulated garlic. Place chicken in bag with flour mixture. Shake until chicken is well coated.

Heat oil in a Magnalite fryer—oil should reach 350 degrees. Place chicken in hot oil. Fry, turning as chicken browns. Heavy parts such as breast, thighs, and legs will take 15 to 20 minutes, wings about 10 to 15 minutes. Drain chicken on paper towels. Yield: 4 servings.

CHICKEN LIVER PATE

1 lb. chicken livers
2 tbsp. melted chicken fat
¼ cup chopped green
  onions
1 rib celery (chopped)
1 tbsp. gelatin
¼ cup water
1 hard-boiled egg (chopped)
1 tbsp. Worcestershire sauce
6 large stuffed olives
  (chopped)
2 dashes Tabasco sauce
½ tsp. salt
½ tsp. cayenne pepper
Whole stuffed olives and
  parsley for garnish

Sauté chicken livers in melted fat with green onions and celery. Cook until livers are done and onions are clear. Mix gelatin in water until well dissolved and add to liver mixture. Stir mixture well to avoid clumps. Cook for 5 minutes on a slow heat.

Add chopped egg, Worcestershire sauce, olives, Tabasco, salt, and cayenne. Mix well. Remove mixture from heat and place in blender in small amounts at a time. Blend until mixture is smooth and creamy. Pour into a mold that has been sprayed with cooking spray. Chill for 3 hours until firm. Unmold and garnish with stuffed olives and parsley.

STEWED HEN IN BROWN GRAVY

1 4-lb. stewing hen
2 tbsp. salt
1 tbsp. black pepper
3 tbsp. vegetable oil
3 tbsp. flour
1 cup chopped onions
½ cup chopped celery
1 cup chopped green
  peppers
4 cups water
1 tbsp. chopped garlic
1 tbsp. chopped parsley
1 tsp. paprika
2 whole red peppers

For this, take out your Dutch oven. Cut hen in serving-size pieces. Season with 1 tablespoon of the salt and the black pepper. Heat oil in pot and add hen. Cover; let steam for about 30 to 35 minutes. Remove from pot. Set aside. In same pot, place flour. Stir and brown flour, stirring constantly.

Add onions, celery, and green peppers; cook until onions are tender. Slowly add water. Add garlic, parsley, and paprika. Stir well; add remaining salt and the whole red peppers. Return hen to pot. Cover and cook over medium heat for 35 to 40 minutes or until hen is tender. This is traditionally served with baked macaroni. Yield: 6 servings.

The Cotton Pickers by H. Strickland

In this age of computers, space shuttles, and life in the fast lane, there is great concern about high blood pressure, high cholesterol, obesity, and many other "no no's." I remember a day when we children would wake up to the great smell of bacon, ham, and eggs, or lunch on a pork chop or oyster sandwich on French bread, and in the evening dine on pork roast and sweet potatoes. Concern about blood pressure did not enter our minds. *Mon chéri,* the term "cholesterol" would have been Greek to us.

By the same token, Mother didn't have her Porsche and Daddy didn't have his Mercedes Benz to take us to and from school. So there was the daily trek to school—about a mile at least. The walk to church on Sundays in our patent leather Sunday shoes (that always hurt) seemed like five miles.

So much for the old struggling days. This is a new day. Progress, progress, progress.

Who knows, in the next century we may be served Shrimp Creole in a capsule. Before it gets to that, I have put together several tasty Creole recipes that are low in sodium and cholesterol. Slow down just a little and enjoy them.

LOW-SODIUM CREOLE
OVEN-FRIED CHICKEN

½ **frying chicken**
White pepper
1 cup flour
¼ **tsp. ground thyme**
½ **tsp. paprika**
¼ **tsp. granulated garlic**

Preheat oven to 375 degrees. Remove skin from chicken, cut chicken in pieces, and season with white pepper. Place flour in bag or bowl. Mix in last three ingredients. Shake chicken in bag in flour mixture. Remove chicken and shake off excess flour. Spray pan with nonstick cooking spray. Place chicken on pan. Bake for 45 minutes. Yield: 2 servings.

POACHED TROUT
WITH ORANGE SAUCE

2 4-oz. trout fillets
White pepper
1 tbsp. flour
1 cup water
1 tbsp. unsalted margarine
Juice from 1 large orange

Season fish with white pepper. Pat fish with flour. Bring the water to a boil in skillet. Shake excess flour from fish. Place fish in boiling water. Turn as fish are cooked on each side. When fish are done (texture should be firm and fish white), remove from skillet carefully. Keep on warm platter.

Put margarine in pan; heat and lightly brown. Add orange juice to margarine. Cook 3 to 4 minutes. Pour over trout. Yield: 2 servings.

CHICKEN BALLS AND
WHOLE WHEAT SPAGHETTI

1 slice toasted wheat bread
1½ cups water
2 7-oz. boneless chicken
    breasts (skinned and
    ground)
1 cup chopped onions
1 tbsp. + 1 tsp. chopped
    garlic
¼ tsp. ground oregano
2 tbsp. chopped parsley
¼ tsp. white pepper
2 tbsp. flour
1 tbsp. corn oil
¼ cup chopped celery
1½ cups chopped fresh
    tomatoes
½ cup burgundy wine
¼ tsp. cayenne pepper
½ cup chopped green
    peppers
½ tsp. oregano leaves
½ tsp. paprika
Whole wheat spaghetti

Put bread in bowl; sprinkle with ½ cup of the water. Mix the chicken with ¼ cup of the chopped onions, 1 teaspoon of the garlic, the ground oregano, 1 teaspoon of the parsley, the white pepper, and the bread (which should have all water squeezed out). Mix well. Shape into balls (should make 4). Dust with 1 tablespoon of the flour, completely covering each chicken ball. Put remaining water in skillet. Bring to a boil. Poach chicken balls in water, turning from time to time. Cook for 5 to 6 minutes. Remove from skillet and reserve water. Set aside.

Heat corn oil in pan. Add remaining flour. Add remaining onions and the celery. Cook until onions are clear. Add tomatoes, the reserved water, and wine. Stir well so there are no lumps in sauce. Add remaining garlic and parsley, and the cayenne pepper, green peppers, oregano leaves, and paprika. Bring to a slow boil. Add chicken balls. Cook slowly for 10 minutes. Serve over whole wheat spaghetti. Yield: 2 to 4 servings.

SHRIMP JAMBALAYA

¼ cup chopped onions
1 cup uncooked rice
¼ cup chopped green
 peppers
1 tsp. chopped garlic
1 tbsp. chopped celery
2 cups water
½ tsp. thyme leaves
½ tsp. cayenne pepper
1 tsp. chopped parsley
½ tsp. paprika
6 raw shrimp (peeled and
 deveined)

Spray saucepan with nonstick cooking spray. Place on medium heat. Sauté onions until clear. Add all other ingredients except shrimp. Stir well. Add shrimp.

Cover very tightly with foil to keep in all steam. Cook on very low heat for 35 minutes. Uncover and toss rice. Cover again and cook very slowly until rice is done.

If you're a lover of jambalaya, you can use this recipe more often by substituting farm-grown catfish for shrimp. Just cut fish in cubes. Yield: 2 servings.

VEAL WITH TOMATOES AND BASIL

1 4-oz. veal cutlet
Black pepper
½ onion (sliced)
¼ green pepper (sliced)
1 ripe medium tomato
  (peeled and chopped)
½ tsp. chopped garlic
1 tbsp. chopped fresh basil
½ tsp. chopped parsley
½ tsp. crushed red pepper

Pound veal very thin (if you don't have a meat tenderizer, the bottom of a bottle will pound the veal perfectly). Sprinkle veal with black pepper. Heat skillet and spray with cooking spray. Place veal in hot skillet. Turn twice. Veal should not take long to cook. Lower heat. Add onions. Cook for 5 minutes. Add green peppers, tomato, garlic, basil, parsley, and crushed red pepper. Let simmer for another 10 minutes.

This recipe will work well with fish also. Substitute redfish or any other sturdy fish for veal. Yield: 1 serving.

BROCCOLI WITH LEMON JUICE

8 oz. broccoli
1 tbsp. sweet, unsalted
  margarine
1 tbsp. lemon juice

Place broccoli in boiling water. Let boil for 5 minutes. Drain. Melt margarine in small skillet. Add lemon juice, whipping constantly for 2 or 3 minutes. Pour over broccoli. Yield: 2 to 4 servings.

LOW-CHOLESTEROL
POTATO SALAD

¼ cup skim milk
½ cup dry curd cottage
  cheese
¼ tsp. celery salt
¼ tsp. dillweed
¼ tsp. dry mustard
2 tbsp. white vinegar
2 tbsp. lemon juice
3 lb. potatoes
½ cup chopped green
  onions
½ cup chopped celery
2 tbsp. chopped parsley
½ tsp. white pepper

Mix skim milk, cottage cheese, celery salt, dillweed, mustard, vinegar, and lemon juice. Place in blender and blend until smooth. Refrigerate for 1 hour.

Scrub potatoes well. Boil in jackets until they are tender. Cool and peel. Cut potatoes in small pieces. Add green onions, celery, parsley, and white pepper. Toss well; pour milk mixture over potatoes and mix well. Chill for 30 minutes. Yield: 4 servings.

LOW-SODIUM CREOLE
RED KIDNEY BEANS

1 lb. red beans
2 qt. water
1 cup chopped onions
½ cup chopped green
   peppers
1 tbsp. chopped garlic
1 tsp. thyme leaves
1 tsp. chopped parsley
1 bay leaf
1 tsp. black pepper

Place beans in pot. Add water and onions. Bring to a boil. Let beans boil for 1 hour or until tender.

Lower heat. Add green pepper and garlic, stirring and mashing some of the beans against side of pot. Add thyme, parsley, bay leaf, and black pepper. Cook beans over low fire for 30 minutes longer or until beans are creamy. Served over boiled rice. Yield: 4 to 6 servings.

Upper Room by John Biggers

Growing up, we had nothing but vegetables. Daddy was a farmer and also worked in the Jahncke Shipyard when there was work to be had. There was a lot of work to be done on the wooden boats they brought in before World War II. That was the big deal other than planting strawberries and vegetables.

Coming up in the depression days, Daddy always planted everything. He planted greens, okra, and onions. I never bought an onion until I came to New Orleans. My daddy supplied everybody with vegetables. I never will forget working in the garden and watching Aunt Teen's house across the way. Aunt Teen and her daughter sat on the front porch every evening. In the country, people would take their baths and sit out on the porch.

Aunt Teen and her daughter would sit out there fanning mosquitos, and we would still be out there watering the onions into the night because you can only water when the sun goes down. We would water and water. As soon as everything came up Daddy would say, "Go give this to Aunt Teen." I would get so aggravated. And he always made us give the best away. "Oh, these nice ripe tomatoes, you give that to…," he would say. We had worked like dogs and they were sitting there all prim and proper the entire time and we had to bring it to them. But that was the way Daddy was. He always said if you give of yourself, it will all come back to you one day.

We always had food because Daddy planted it. Sometimes the vegetables were prepared without all of the seasoning meat. My mother cooked a lot with onions and she did a pretty good job with those things. She didn't have all of the fancy spices.

If you have ever grown vegetables yourself, you don't care if you grow another one in your life. I'd just as soon go down to the French Market and buy it off of some vendor. Some of my sisters still grow herbs for me, but I don't care if I never grow another thing. Farming has got to be the hardest thing in the world. Having grown vegetables does make you more conscious of the quality of the things you are buying, though. There is nothing like fresh vegetables. The taste is totally different from processed ones.

Needless to say, I know of many ways to cook vegetables. Any of these recipes should help round out a meal, or can become the main attraction itself!

RED BEANS

In Madisonville, where I grew up, we would use smoked ham to add flavor to our red beans. In New Orleans they would use pickled meat. Pickling of pork was done in the Creole community. Pickled ribs with potato salad were popular. The meat was pickled in a brine, more or less, along with seasonings. There is a market in New Orleans that still makes pickled meat, in just this way. They might also use some kind of vinegar. In this red beans recipe, I stick with the smoked meats, just like in the country.

1 lb. red kidney beans
2 qt. water
1 large onion (chopped)
¼ cup vegetable oil
1 lb. smoked ham (cubed)
1 lb. smoked sausage (in
    ½-inch slices)
1 cup water
1 tbsp. chopped garlic
1 bay leaf
1 tbsp. black pepper
2 tbsp. chopped parsley
1 tsp. whole thyme leaves
2 level tbsp. salt

Pick through beans, removing all bad beans or any other particles. Wash beans well. Place beans in 5-quart pot. Add the 2 quarts of water. Add onions; bring to a boil. Lower heat and let beans boil slowly for 1 hour. When beans are soft stir well, mashing some against side of pot.

Heat oil in frying pan; add ham and sausage. Sauté in oil for 5 minutes. Then add the sausage, ham, and oil to beans. Deglaze pan with the cup of water, then pour into beans. Add all other ingredients. Let simmer for 30 minutes. Beans should be nice and creamy. Serve over rice. Yield: 6 servings.

WHITE BEANS WITH COLLARDS

1 lb. large navy beans
2 qt. water
1 large onion (chopped)
1 small bunch collard greens
1 lb. smoked ham (cubed)
3 cloves garlic (chopped)
1 tbsp. salt
1 tbsp. white pepper
1 whole red pepper
½ cup vegetable oil
1 bay leaf

In a Magnalite stockpot place well-washed beans, water, and onion. Bring beans to a boil and boil for 1 hour. Remove all large stems from greens. Wash greens thoroughly. Cut into strips, then cut strips of greens into squares. Add greens to beans along with ham, garlic, salt, white pepper, and whole red pepper. Stir well, adding vegetable oil and bay leaf. Cover pot and let simmer for 30 minutes until both greens and beans are tender. Yield: 6 servings.

STUFFED TURNIPS

6 medium turnips
Water to cover
2 tsp. salt
1 lb. pork sausage
¼ cup chopped onions
1 clove garlic (mashed and
chopped)
1 tbsp. chopped parsley
½ tsp. cayenne pepper
½ cup bread crumbs
Butter

Remove tops and roots from turnips. Peel turnips and place in large Dutch oven. Cover turnips with water and add 1 teaspoon of the salt. Bring to a boil and cook for 10 minutes until turnips are tender. Remove turnips from water and set aside.

Sauté sausage, onions, and garlic; cook until onions are soft. With a teaspoon, scoop out middle of turnips leaving ¼-inch shells. Add middle of turnips to sausage mixture, mashing together well. Add parsley, cayenne, and remaining salt. Cook for 10 minutes.

Add ¼ cup of the bread crumbs and mix well. Remove from heat and fill turnip shells with sausage mixture. Sprinkle tops of filled shells with remaining bread crumbs. Dot tops with butter. Bake for 10 minutes in 375-degree oven. Yield: 6 servings.

BEAN CAKES
WITH HOT CHILI SAUCE

1 lb. dried black-eyed peas
1½ qt. water
1 onion (diced)
3 cloves garlic
1 bay leaf
2 sprigs fresh thyme
1 tsp. salt
1 ham hock
1 cup flour
4 cups peanut oil

Pick through beans, then wash beans thoroughly. Put beans to boil in water. Add all other ingredients except flour and oil. Bring to a hard boil and boil for 20 minutes. Lower heat and cook until beans are soft. All liquid should be just about out. Remove the ham hock.

Drain beans and reserve 1 cup liquid. Place beans in a blender, adding a little liquid. Blend to a paste consistency. Flour hands and shape bean mixture into round flat cakes. Heat peanut oil in heavy frying pan. Fry cakes until brown and crispy on outside. Serve with Hot Chili Sauce. Yield: 8 cakes.

HOT CHILI SAUCE
1 cup chopped onions
2 tbsp. olive oil
1 tsp. chopped garlic
1 tbsp. chopped chives
1½ cups whole tomatoes
   (crushed)
3 tbsp. hot chili sauce (can
   be found in Oriental food
   stores)
1 tsp. lemon juice
1 cup water

Sauté onions in olive oil for 3 to 4 minutes. Add garlic and chives. Stir well. Add tomatoes, chili sauce, lemon juice, and water. Simmer for 15 minutes on a slow heat.

TURNIPS AND GREEN PEAS
IN CREAM SAUCE

3 cups diced turnips
Water to cover
Salt
1 cup fresh or frozen green
   peas
¼ lb. butter
2 tbsp. flour
2 cups milk
½ tsp. white pepper
½ cup plain bread crumbs
½ cup grated Romano
   cheese

Place turnips in pot and cover with water. Add salt and boil for 10 minutes. Add green peas. Bring to a boil, cooking for 5 minutes. Remove from heat and drain off water. Pour into a baking dish and set aside.

Heat butter in saucepan; add flour, stirring constantly. Do not brown, just let the flour dissolve in the butter. Slowly add milk, stirring as it is added. Add white pepper; stir and cook until thick and creamy. Pour over turnips and peas. Mix bread crumbs with Romano cheese and sprinkle over top of casserole. Bake for 20 minutes in preheated oven (375 degrees). Yield: 6 servings.

STUFFED MIRLITONS
(Chayote Squash)

6 large mirlitons
Water
½ cup butter
½ lb. smoked ham (ground)
1 cup chopped onions
1 lb. shrimp (peeled,
   deveined, and chopped)
¼ cup chopped green onions
2 cloves garlic (mashed and
   chopped)
1 tsp. salt
1 tbsp. chopped parsley
1 tsp. white pepper
1¼ cups plain bread crumbs
¼ tsp. paprika

Cut mirlitons in half and remove seeds. Place in pot of water; boil for 15 minutes or until tender. Drain off water and let cool.

Scoop out the pulpy inside of mirlitons, keeping shells intact; set aside.

Melt butter in pot. Add ham and onions, cooking until onions are soft. Add chopped shrimp and stir well. Add mirliton pulp to mixture, mashing as it is added. Add green onions, garlic, salt, parsley, and white pepper. Let cook for 20 to 30 minutes. Mixture might be a bit watery at this point. Tighten mixture with 1 cup of the bread crumbs. Fill the mirliton shells with the mixture.

Toss together the remaining ¼ cup of bread crumbs and paprika. Sprinkle this mixture over each filled shell. Bake in preheated oven at 375 degrees for 15 minutes. Yield: 12 servings.

MIRLITON WITH CHICKEN

5 medium mirlitons
2 chicken breasts (boned
  and skinned)
2 chicken thighs (boned
  and skinned)
1 tbsp. salt
1 tsp. white pepper
¼ cup flour
¼ lb. butter
½ cup chopped onions
½ cup chopped celery
1 clove garlic (mashed and
  chopped)
½ tsp. ground thyme

    Peel mirlitons, remove seeds, cut into small cubes, and set aside. Cut breasts and thighs in half. Season chicken with salt and white pepper. Dredge chicken in flour. Shake off excess flour. Melt butter in large skillet, being careful not to burn it. Place chicken in hot butter, cooking slowly on all sides. Brown chicken just slightly.

    Add onions and celery, turning as you cook. Let onions get clear (not brown). Add diced mirlitons to chicken mixture. Add garlic and thyme, stirring lightly. Cover and cook over medium heat for 20 minutes or until mirlitons are tender. This dish is great with saffron or yellow rice. Yield: 4 to 6 servings.

PICKLED MIRLITON

8 large mirlitons (diced)
10 medium onions (sliced)
2 green peppers (diced)
Cold water and ice cubes to
  cover
½ cup salt
5 cups vinegar
5 cups sugar
½ tsp. tumeric
½ tsp. ground cloves
2 tbsp. mustard seeds
2 tbsp. celery seeds

In a large bowl, combine mirlitons, onions, and green peppers. Cover with cold water and ice cubes; let stand for three hours. Drain well. Boil remaining ingredients then add vegetable mixture. Cook over low heat for 5 minutes. Pour into Mason jars. Fill jars with liquid and seal. Allow vegetable to age several weeks on shelf for best flavoring. Yield: 2 to 3 pints.

FRIED SQUASH

2 young tender white
  squash
Salt and white pepper
1 cup Pet milk
4 eggs (beaten)
Oil for frying
Bread crumbs

Peel squash and cut in half. Remove all large seeds. Cut halves in thin slices. Season squash with salt and white pepper. Pour the milk into the beaten eggs and whisk together. Pour egg mixture over squash and let soak for 3 minutes while heating oil in heavy skillet. Dredge squash in bread crumbs, coating both sides well, then place in hot oil. Fry until squash is tender and brown, about 10 minutes. Yield: 4 servings.

STEWED OKRA
WITH HAM AND SHRIMP

¼ cup bacon drippings or
    vegetable oil
½ lb. smoked ham (cubed)
½ cup chopped onions
½ cup chopped celery
1½ lb. okra (cut in ½-inch
    pieces)
2 cups whole tomatoes
    (crushed)
1 cup water
1 tsp. salt
½ tsp. cayenne pepper
1 cup chopped green
    pepper
½ lb. shrimp (peeled and
deveined)

Heat drippings or oil in 3-quart saucepot. Add ham and fry for 3 to 4 minutes. Add onions and celery and cook until onions wilt. Add okra, tomatoes, water, salt, and cayenne; stir gently. Cover and cook over medium heat for 20 minutes. Add green pepper and shrimp. Mix well into okra, taking care not to break okra. Place lid on pot and cook until shrimp are just tender, about 5 minutes. Yield: 4 to 6 servings.

CROWDER PEAS WITH OKRA

1 large ham hock
2 qt. water
4 cups fresh shelled
  crowder peas
1 onion (chopped)
1 green pepper (chopped)
1 sprig fresh thyme
1 bay leaf
¼ cup bacon drippings or
  vegetable oil
½ lb. smoke sausage (sliced)
1 tbsp. flour
1 tbsp. salt
1 tbsp. black pepper
2 cloves garlic (chopped)
6 to 8 small okra (tops
  removed)

In a 5-quart pot place ham hock and the water. Let boil for 30 minutes. Add peas, onions, green peppers, thyme, and bay leaf. Lower heat and boil slowly for 20 minutes until peas are soft. In a skillet, heat bacon drippings. Cook sausage in drippings for about 3 to 4 minutes; sprinkle flour over sausage and stir well, scraping bottom of skillet. Pour a little water in skillet to deglaze. Pour sausage mixture into peas. Add salt, black pepper, garlic, and okra. Cover pot and let simmer slowly for 15 minutes—okra should be just tender. Serve over rice. Yield: 4 servings.

STEWED OKRA WITH TOMATOES

I don't see why anybody in New Orleans should go hungry. It seems to me they could just go to the French Market in the Quarter and pick up everything that the vendors are throwing away. You could take all of those soft tomatoes and make the best stewed tomatoes. Mix them with a little butter and add some basil leaves and there you go. Or add them to stewed okra. You can really cook a lot with just a little imagination.

¼ cup margarine
½ cup chopped onions
3 lb. cut fresh or frozen
   okra
½ cup chopped green
   peppers
2 cups whole tomatoes
1 level tbsp. salt
½ tsp. cayenne pepper
1 tsp. whole thyme
¼ cup chopped celery
1 tsp. chopped garlic

Melt margarine in 2- to 3-quart saucepan. Add onions and stir until onions are clear. Add okra, green peppers, and tomatoes. Cook over medium heat for 10 minutes. Add salt, cayenne, thyme, celery, and garlic. Stir mixture and let cook for about 25 minutes more or until okra are just tender. Do not overcook (okra will become mushy). Yield: 6 servings.

SPINACH PIE

3 lb. fresh spinach
¼ cup extra virgin olive oil
2 tbsp. flour
2 tbsp. chopped green
  onions
½ tsp. chopped garlic
½ cup Pet milk
½ cup water
3 tbsp. chopped hot
  jalapeno peppers
½ lb. Monterey Jack cheese
  (grated)
½ tsp. salt
5 strips bacon (crisply fried
  and crumbled)
Phyllo dough

Remove large stems from spinach and wash thoroughly. Boil spinach until tender. Drain and chop spinach. Set aside.

Heat olive oil over medium heat. Add flour and stir well. Add green onions and garlic. Cook for about 3 minutes; slowly add milk and water. Stir until smooth. Add peppers, cheese, and salt; mix well. Mixture should be creamy. Spray square glass baking dish with cooking spray. Put in layer of spinach and layer of cream mixture. Sprinkle with bacon. Last layer should be spinach. Top with phyllo dough. Bake in 375-degree oven until dough is light brown, about 20 minutes. Yield: 4 to 6 servings.

CREAMED SPINACH

2 lb. fresh or 2 10-oz. pkg.
frozen chopped spinach
¼ cup water
1 tsp. salt
1 tbsp. butter
1 tbsp. flour
½ cup Pet milk
1 egg (beaten)
¼ tsp. ground nutmeg

Place spinach in boiling water; add salt. Boil spinach until tender, about 15 to 20 minutes. Drain spinach in colander.

In a small pot, heat butter. Add flour and stir well—be sure it does not brown. Cook for 5 minutes. Slowly add milk, stirring as you add. Add egg and nutmeg and whisk briskly.

Place spinach in bowl, pour sauce over spinach, and mix well. Place spinach in casserole dish and place in warm oven until serving time. Yield: 4 servings.

SWEET POTATOES

My family used to get teased a lot about sweet potatoes when I was growing up. They said we ate sweet potatoes like other people ate bread. We did. My daddy grew sweet potatoes so that was what we had. Even today, some of my sisters won't have them because we ate them so often. One sister says all she can do with a sweet potato is put it in her pocket and keep her hands warm, like we used to do on the way to school. We didn't have gloves in the depression, so you had to think of something. But my daddy was right. Sweet potatoes are really meant to be enjoyed at the dinner table.

3 lb. sweet potatoes
1½ cups sugar
2 tbsp. butter
1 tsp. cinnamon
1½ cups water

Wash and peel sweet potatoes. Cut potatoes into ½-inch sticks. In a small Dutch oven place potatoes and sugar. Cut in butter and add cinnamon and water. Cover pot and place on medium heat. Cook for 20 minutes or until potatoes are tender. Yield: 4 to 6 servings.

GREAT SWEET POTATOES

4 large sweet potatoes
½ cup sugar
½ cup condensed milk
½ cup chopped pecans
1 tsp. cinnamon
¼ cup melted butter
Juice from 1 medium
  orange
Marshmallows

Boil sweet potatoes until tender. Let cool. Peel potatoes. Place potatoes in large mixing bowl and mash well. Add sugar, condensed milk, pecans, cinnamon, butter, and orange juice. With a wire whisk, whip potatoes until smooth. Place potatoes in a greased baking dish and top with marshmallows. Bake in 375-degree oven until marshmallows melt and brown slightly, 15 to 20 minutes. Yield: 6 servings.

SWEET POTATO DRESSING

½ cup chopped green
   onions
½ cup chopped celery
½ cup melted butter
3 medium sweet potatoes
   (boiled and mashed)
¼ tsp. cayenne pepper
1 tsp. salt
¼ tsp. thyme
¼ tsp. rosemary
⅛ tsp. sage
Pinch of mace
1 tsp. chopped parsley
1 egg (beaten)
1½ cups bread crumbs

Sauté green onions and celery in melted butter. Add mashed sweet potatoes, cayenne pepper, salt, thyme, rosemary, sage, mace, chopped parsley, and egg. Mix well; tighten with bread crumbs. Bake in 350-degree oven for 15 to 20 minutes. Excellent with roast pork or fowl. Yield: 6 servings.

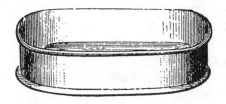

CORN PUDDING

**6 to 8 ears tender white
  corn
1 cup sugar
6 eggs (well beaten)
2 12-oz. cans Pet milk
1 cup water
1 tsp. vanilla
1 tbsp. butter**

Clean corn thoroughly, removing all silk. Grate corn from cob. With the back of a knife scrape the cob to remove the remaining pulp; set aside. Mix sugar, eggs, milk, water, and vanilla well. Pour the grated corn in the egg mixture. Butter a glass baking dish. Pour corn mixture in baking dish and place in a 300-degree oven. Bake about 30 to 40 minutes until pudding is golden and appears to be a thick custard. Yield: 4 to 6 servings.

FRIED CORN

**12 ears fresh corn
6 strips bacon
1 tsp. salt
1 tsp. white pepper
½ cup chopped green
  onions**

Clean corn and wash thoroughly with vegetable brush. Be sure to remove all silk. Cut corn from cob. Be sure not to cut too close to cob. With back of knife, scrape cobs well. Add scraping to corn; set aside.

Cut bacon in small pieces. Place bacon in hot skillet; cook until brown. Remove bacon and set aside, reserving drippings. Heat bacon drippings in a Magnalite Dutch oven. Add corn, salt, white pepper, and green onions. Stir and cook on high heat for 10 minutes. Add bacon and cook for another 5 minutes. Corn should be tender and crunchy. Great as a breakfast dish. Yield: 6 servings.

SUCCOTASH

¼ cup vegetable oil
1 lb. smoked ham (cubed)
1 large onion (chopped)
Kernels from 6 ears corn or
    1 10-oz. pkg. cut corn
2 to 3 lb. lima beans or
    1 10-oz. pkg. baby lima
    beans
2 cups water
1 large green pepper
    (chopped)
2 cloves garlic (finely
    chopped)
1 tbsp. salt
1 tsp. white pepper
1½ lb. cubed okra or 1
    10-oz. pkg. cut okra
2 whole tomatoes
    (quartered)

Heat oil in large pot and fry ham for 5 minutes. Add onions, corn, and shelled lima beans; stir well. Add water and cook over medium heat for 10 minutes. Add green peppers, garlic, salt, and white pepper. Stir in okra and tomatoes and let simmer for 20 minutes until okra are tender. Yield: 4 to 6 servings.

ITALIAN SALAD

½ head of lettuce
½ cup broken olives with
  pimentos
1 tsp. capers
¼ cup sliced celery
6 pitted ripe olives
¼ lb. diced salami
1 medium tomato (cut in
  eighths)
½ tsp. salt
½ tsp. coarsely ground
  black pepper
½ cup olive oil
¼ cup vinegar
4 pieces of anchovies

Clean lettuce well. Break lettuce in a bowl. Add broken olives, capers, celery, ripe olives, and salami. Toss lightly and add tomatoes, salt, and pepper. Pour olive oil and vinegar over mixture; toss gently. Garnish with anchovies. Yield: 2 servings.

POTATO SALAD

When I finished high school, and before I came to work in the laundry in New Orleans, I worked for a lady in Madisonville who had a boardinghouse. The place had only men—I always seem to be in places where there are only men—who worked at the shipyard and boarded at her place. They would come home at noon and we would have to cook lunch. She taught me how to cook a few things. There was another black girl working there and we used to laugh together because this woman cooked so different. She used to cook string beans and tell us that we needed to cook a roux for these string beans. We would laugh and laugh.

We cooked on this great big wood stove. When we did make a roux, we would take the lid off of the stove to make it in a hurry over the open fire. Many times we burned up the roux and would have to pour it in the fire.

One of the things I learned there was how to make potato salad. The lady didn't put mayonnaise in it—she used chicken fat. She raised her own chickens until they were six weeks old and then we killed them. We'd have to clean them and fry them. To make it easier, though, this recipe uses mayonnaise!

> **4 medium white potatoes**
> **1 tsp. salt**
> **½ tsp. white pepper**
> **3 hard-boiled eggs**
> **(chopped)**
> **1 cup chopped celery**
> **1 tbsp. chopped parsley**
> **1 tbsp. chopped dill pickles**
> **1 tbsp. yellow mustard**
> **½ cup mayonnaise**
> **Lettuce leaf**

Boil potatoes in their jackets. Drain and let potatoes cool. Peel and cut potatoes in small pieces. Season potatoes with salt and white pepper. Add all other ingredients and mix well. Chill for about a half-hour. Serve on lettuce leaf. Yield: 4 to 6 servings.

OKRA SALAD

12 small tender okra
Pinch of salt
¼ cup oil
⅓ cup vinegar
½ tsp. salt
½ tsp. black pepper

Wash okra well and cut off stem ends. Place okra in boiling water and add a pinch of salt. Let okra boil slowly and cook until tender— about 20 minutes. Do not overcook. Drain okra in colander and cool. Lay okra on serving dish. Put oil, vinegar, the ½ teaspoon of salt, and the pepper in bowl; beat well with a wire whisk. Pour over okra. Serve chilled. Yield: 3 to 4 servings.

CARROT AND RAISIN SALAD

2 cups shredded carrots
¼ cup pineapple juice
½ cup raisins
5 tbsp. mayonnaise
Lettuce leaf

In a mixing bowl, place all ingredients (except lettuce leaf) and mix well. Chill for 30 minutes. Serve on lettuce leaf. Yield: 4 servings.

VEGETABLE SALAD

6 medium new potatoes
Water to cover
1 whole carrot (scraped
   and diced)
½ cup fresh or frozen cut
   string beans
½ cup fresh or frozen
   green peas
¼ cup chopped celery
¼ tsp. dillweed
1 small red apple (cored
   and diced)
½ tsp. salt
½ tsp. white pepper
Mayonnaise

With vegetable brush, scrub new potatoes well. Place potatoes in pot and cover with water. Boil potatoes until tender. Drain off water and let cool. Place diced carrots in small pot of water. Let boil for 5 minutes. Add cut string beans and peas; let boil for 5 minutes. Drain off water and let cool. When cool, cut potatoes in pieces (do not peel). Add cooked vegetables, celery, dillweed, apple, salt, and white pepper. Add mayonnaise to taste. Toss salad well. Let chill. Yield: 4 servings.

LEAH'S COLE SLAW

Cole slaw is a must for Fourth of July picnics. I am always sure to bring some to serve with the baked ham, hot dogs, hamburgers, and potato salad.

½ **head of small cabbage**
   (chopped, not shredded)
¼ **cup shredded carrots**
¼ **cup mayonnaise**
3 **tbsp. pineapple juice**
1 **tsp. chopped parsley**
½ **cup pineapple chunks**
2 **tbsp. sugar**
¼ **tsp. white pepper**
¼ **tsp. salt**
Lettuce leaf

In a large mixing bowl, place all ingredients except lettuce leaf. Mix together well until sugar and salt are dissolved. Chill for 30 minutes and serve on lettuce leaf. Yield: 4 servings.

BEET AND ONION SALAD

4 **large fresh beets**
1 **medium red onion (sliced**
   thin)
1 **tbsp. sweet relish**
½ **tsp. salt**
½ **tsp. black pepper**
½ **tsp. sugar**
¼ **cup vegetable oil**
¼ **cup white vinegar**
Lettuce leaf

Boil beets until tender. Let cool. Peel and slice beets. Place sliced beets in a bowl and cover with sliced onion. Add relish, salt, pepper, and sugar. Mix well. Pour oil and vinegar over mixture and toss. Let chill; serve on lettuce leaf. Yield: 4 servings.

VEGETABLE CASSEROLE

2 **eggs (well beaten)**
1½ **cups Pet milk**
1½ **cups water**
1 **tsp. salt**
½ **tsp. white pepper**
1 **cup cooked green peas**
1 **cup chopped boiled**
   carrots
1 **cup cooked green beans**
   (cut in ½-inch pieces)
½ **stick butter**
2 **cups seasoned bread**
   crumbs

Mix beaten eggs with milk and water. Add salt and white pepper. Beat the mixture well.

Mix peas, carrots, and green beans. In greased casserole dish add a layer of vegetables, thin slices of butter, and sprinkle generously with seasoned bread crumbs. Repeat this procedure until all vegetables are used. Pour milk and egg mixture over casserole, sprinkle with remaining bread crumbs and butter, and bake in a 350-degree oven for about 35 minutes until mixture is firm. Yield: 4 servings.

STUFFED TOMATOES

6 tomatoes
1 cup boiling water
½ cup uncooked long-grain
   rice
2 tbsp. chopped celery
1 tbsp. butter
1 tsp. chopped garlic
2 hard-boiled egg yolks
   (mashed)
¼ cup milk
¼ cup bread crumbs
¼ tsp. thyme
¼ tsp. curry powder
½ tsp. white pepper
1 tsp. parsley

Cut tops from tomatoes and remove pulp. In a 1-quart saucepot, boil water then add rice and tomato pulp. Cook until rice is tender. In a skillet, sauté celery in butter; add garlic. Stir for 4 minutes. Add mashed egg yolks. Stir well; add milk and bread crumbs. Stir, add seasonings, toss rice mixture into seasonings, and stir well. Stuff tomatoes, replace the tops, and place tomatoes in a baking dish. Bake at 350 degrees until tomatoes are soft—20 to 25 minutes. Yield: 6 servings.

STUFFED ONIONS

**6 medium white onions
(peeled)
Boiling water
2 tbsp. margarine
½ lb. ground chuck
½ lb. hot sausage meat
1 tsp. chopped garlic
1 tbsp. chopped parsley
½ tsp. ground thyme
½ tsp. salt
¼ tsp. cayenne pepper
2 cups cooked yellow rice
Bread crumbs and butter
for topping**

Place peeled onions in boiling water. Boil for 10 minutes. Remove onions from water and cool. With a grapefruit knife, remove insides from onions, leaving ¼-inch shell. Chop insides of onions and set aside. In heavy skillet melt margarine; add ground meat and sausage meat. Mix meats together well while cooking.

Add chopped insides of onions, garlic, parsley, thyme, salt, and cayenne pepper. Cook for 15 minutes. Add rice to mixture and mix well. Stuff mixture into onion shells. Sprinkle tops with bread crumbs and drizzle with butter. Bake in shallow baking pan for 20 minutes in a 350-degree oven. Yield: 6 servings.

FRENCH-STYLE STRING BEANS
WITH HAM AND POTATOES

½ cup margarine
2 lb. smoked ham (cubed)
1½ cups chopped onions
2 cups water
½ tsp. salt
¼ tsp. cayenne pepper
6 small red potatoes
3 lb. fresh or frozen
   French-cut string beans

In a 2½-quart saucepan, place margarine. Put pan over heat and add ham. Let ham cook for 10 minutes, turning often. Add onions; stir and cook until clear. Add water, salt, and cayenne pepper. Lower heat. Scrub potatoes well with vegetable brush. With a paring knife, cut a band of skin from around each potato. Place potatoes in pan with ham and onions. Let cook for 10 minutes until potatoes are just beginning to get soft. Add string beans. Stir mixture, cover pot, and let cook until beans and potatoes are done, about 10 minutes. Important not to overcook, since it will cause beans to become mushy. Yield: 6 servings.

PASTA PRINTEMPS

1 lb. spinach fettucine
½ cup cut green beans
6 broccoli florets
6 cauliflower florets
½ cup diced carrots
1 cup milk
1 tbsp. cornstarch
½ tsp. salt
¼ tsp. white pepper
1 tbsp. butter
Paprika and parsley for
  garnish

Boil fettucine according to package directions. Drain and set aside. Place all washed vegetables in a steamer. Steam for 6 minutes. Mix 1 tablespoon of milk with cornstarch. Add cornstarch to remaining milk. Heat milk mixture slowly. Add salt, pepper, and butter. Whisk mixture until smooth. Mix pasta and vegetables in a casserole dish. Pour sauce over entire dish. Bake in 375-degree oven for 15 minutes. Sprinkle with paprika and parsley. Yield: 4 servings.

MUSTARD GREENS WITH
PICKLED PORK AND POTATOES

2 lb. pickled pork (cubed)
2 qt. water
4 bunches mustard greens
Water to cover greens
½ cup chopped onions
1 whole red pepper
1 bay leaf
2 medium white potatoes
  (quartered)

Place pickled pork in pot and cover with water. Let boil until meat is tender. While meat is boiling, remove all large stems from greens. Wash thoroughly, changing water two or three times.

Place greens in large pot, just covering with water. Bring to a boil; let boil for 10 minutes. Drain greens, saving 2 cups of the liquid. Cut greens three or four times. Return greens to pot; add onions, whole red pepper, bay leaf, potatoes, and the 2 cups of liquid. Remove meat from water and add meat to the greens with 1 cup of liquid from pot. Cook for 30 minutes until potatoes are tender and all seasonings have blended.

Note: No salt is added because pickled pork is quite salty. By adding the cup of liquid from the meat, an ample amount of salt is provided as well as enough "pot liquor" (the name used for the liquid in which greens are cooked). Yield: 6 servings.

STEWED EGGPLANT WITH CORN

3 ears corn
2 large eggplants
Water to cover
3 tbsp. vegetable oil
½ lb. smoked ham
½ cup chopped onions
1 large ripe tomato
1 tsp. salt
½ tsp. cayenne pepper
¼ tsp. paprika
¼ tsp. ground thyme
1 clove garlic (mashed and
    chopped)
1 tbsp. chopped parsley

Shuck corn, removing all silk. Wash thoroughly with vegetable brush. Cut corn off cob and set aside. Peel and cube eggplants. Put in pan, cover with water, and let soak for 30 minutes. Place vegetable oil in pot; add ham. Sauté ham over medium heat for 10 minutes. Add onions. Stir well.

Drain water off eggplants, discarding water. Add eggplants to ham and onion mixture. Cover and let cook for 15 minutes. Dip tomato in boiling water so that the entire surface of the tomato is submerged for a short time. Remove immediately and peel off outer skin. Chop tomato and add to eggplants. Stir well, adding salt, cayenne, paprika, thyme, garlic, and parsley. Stir in corn and cook for 15 minutes or until corn is tender. Yield: 6 servings.

EGGPLANT FARCI

2 medium eggplants
¼ lb. butter
1 lb. shrimp (peeled,
   deveined, and chopped)
1 cup chopped onions
1 tbsp. chopped garlic
1 tbsp. chopped parsley
1 tbsp. salt
½ tsp. cayenne pepper
½ lb. white crab meat
½ tsp. whole thyme leaves
1½ cups seasoned bread
   crumbs

Cut eggplants in half. With a tablespoon, scoop out the insides carefully, leaving about ¼-inch-thick shells. Cut insides into small cubes; soak in water for 20 to 30 minutes. Soak shells in separate pan of water. Drain water off eggplant cubes.

In a deep pot, melt the butter and add eggplant cubes, shrimp, and onions. Cover and cook over medium heat for 40 minutes. Remove cover and add garlic, parsley, salt, and cayenne. Stir well. Shrimp and eggplants give off quite a bit of water. Cook long enough to reduce as much of the juices as possible.

Add well-picked crab meat and cook for 10 minutes longer to blend in crab meat. Remove from heat and add bread crumbs; mix well. Stuff well-drained shells with eggplant mixture. Place in baking pan and sprinkle with more bread crumbs. Dot the tops with butter. Bake in preheated oven at 350 degrees for 20 minutes. Yield: 4 servings.

RICE QUENELLES

4 tbsp. flour
4 tbsp. melted butter
1½ cups milk
3 eggs (beaten)
½ tsp. salt
½ tsp. white pepper
½ tsp. cayenne pepper
½ tsp. granulated garlic
3 cups cooked rice
Flour for coating
1½ pt. water

Make white sauce by mixing flour in melted butter and cooking on low heat. Add milk and stir until smooth. Add beaten eggs to sauce. Whisk well and add salt, white pepper, cayenne, and granulated garlic. Mix well. Add rice to sauce. Let mixture cool in refrigerator.

When mixture is cool enough to handle, place flour for coating on a sheet pan. Shape mixture into little log-shaped rolls—about 2 inches long and ½ inch in diameter. Roll in flour, coating well. Set aside. Put the water in a frying pan and bring to a boil. Place quenelles in boiling water and cook, turning often until light brown (about 10 minutes). Yield: 6 to 8 servings.

BAKED RICE

¼ cup melted chicken fat
3 tbsp. flour
½ cup Pet milk
½ cup water
½ tsp. salt
1 tsp. white pepper
1½ cups grated cheddar
   cheese
3 cups cooked rice
Seasoned bread crumbs
½ stick butter
Paprika

Heat chicken fat in pan, add flour, and cook for 5 minutes. Add milk and water, stirring well. Add salt, white pepper, and grated cheese. Continue to stir until cheese is melted and sauce is smooth. Place rice in buttered baking dish. Mix some of the sauce with the rice. Pour remaining sauce over rice. Sprinkle with bread crumbs. Crumble butter over crumbs. Sprinkle with paprika. Bake in 375-degree oven for 30 minutes until sauce is slightly brown. Yield: 6 to 8 servings.

SPINACH RICE

2 bunches or bags of
   spinach
Water to cover
2 tbsp. butter
2 cups rice
1 tsp. salt
Bread crumbs

Remove large stems from spinach. Wash greens thoroughly. Put spinach to boil in just enough water to cover the spinach. Boil for 15 minutes. Drain water off spinach and reserve liquid. Chop spinach and set aside. Place butter in 2-quart saucepot and add rice, 3 cups of reserved spinach liquid (if there is not enough complete with tap water), and salt. Cover pot tightly and cook on a slow heat until rice is tender. Add spinach to rice and mix well. Turn into a casserole dish. Sprinkle top with small amount of bread crumbs. Bake for 20 minutes in 350-degree oven. Yield: 4 servings.

FIESTA RICE

2 tbsp. olive oil
¼ cup chopped carrots
½ cup chopped celery
2 cups rice
¼ cup stuffed olives
¼ cup sliced ripe olives
1 tsp. salt
½ tsp. cayenne pepper
1 tbsp. chopped parsley
¼ tsp. tumeric
3 cups water

Put olive oil in 3-quart saucepot. Add carrots and celery. Stir; add remaining ingredients except water and stir well. Add water and mix well. Place a tight cover on pot and cook on a slow heat for 40 minutes. When rice is tender, fluff with fork to mix well. Yield: 4 servings.

VEGETABLE LOAF

½ cup cooked green peas
½ cup cooked string beans
½ cup chopped boiled
   carrots
1½ cups milk
1 egg (slightly beaten)
1 cup soft bread crumbs
½ tsp. salt
⅛ tsp. pepper
½ tsp. paprika

Toss all vegetables together. Add remaining ingredients. Pour into a greased baking dish (5" x 8") and bake at 350 degrees until firm—35 to 40 minutes. Yield: 4 servings.

Untitled by David Driskell

My mother liked to bake. I don't. I don't do it well because you have to be right on target. I think that is where baking and I fall apart. When it comes to cooking, I know every inch of that gumbo pot. I am going to know every ingredient that goes in there and just how much of it. You can judge once you work with it enough. One day maybe I will be a good baker too if I get the time. I would like to make nice things. Maybe I don't make desserts much because I don't like them. I don't like to lose the taste in my mouth to something sweet. The only sweet thing I really like a lot is chocolate. This desserts section should have something for everyone though, from fruits to pies to cakes.

LEMON SURPRISE

16 oz. cream cheese
2 cups self-rising flour
1 cup butter
3 cups whipping cream
6 oz. instant lemon gelatin
1 cup confectioners' sugar
1 cup chopped pecans
1½ cups whipped cream
1 cup coconut flakes

Preheat oven at 300 degrees. In a large bowl, mix 8 oz. cream cheese, the flour, and the butter. Mix well until a dough consistency is formed. Spread into a 9" x 13½" baking dish. Bake at 300 degrees for 15 minutes or until light brown. Remove from oven and cool. In a chilled mixing bowl, whip the whipping cream and gelatin to a thick custard; set aside in refrigerator.

In a bowl, mix remaining cream cheese and the confectioners' sugar. Spread this mixture over the cooled dough. Then sprinkle the chopped nuts over the cream cheese mixture. Remove the lemon custard from the refrigerator and layer over the nuts. Spread the whipped cream over the lemon custard and top with coconut flakes. Return dish to the refrigerator and chill for 1 hour. Yield: 8 to 10 servings.

LEMON MERINGUE PIE

When I got that first restaurant job at the Colonial Restaurant, all of my aunts and uncles here in New Orleans got together and were going to sit me down and have a talk with me to straighten me out. At the time, the only city work a girl my age and color was expected to do was in the clothes factories. But I got to keep my job.

I made seven dollars a week waiting tables there, and could keep all of my tips. I loved the French Quarter and loved working there. I met so many interesting people. The owner of the Colonial Restaurant and later the Coffee Pot, Mrs. Bessie Sauveur, really taught me to like this city and this business. I still serve the lemon meringue pie she taught me how to make.

1 flaky pie crust (recipe below)
14 oz. condensed milk
3 eggs (separated)
Juice of 3 lemons
¾ cup sugar

FLAKY PIE CRUST
1½ cups plain flour
1¼ tsp. salt
½ cup cold shortening
Cold water

Sift flour and salt. Cut in shortening with pastry knife to get a crumble effect. Add cold water until stiff dough ball is formed. Place dough on floured table and roll out into a thin circle (large enough to fit a 9-inch pie pan). Place dough in pan and pinch edges. Prick pie crust with fork to prevent bubbles when baking. Bake pie crust until brown. Remove from oven and cool.

FILLING

In a bowl, mix condensed milk and egg yolks. Add the lemon juice and fold into mixture until all juice is absorbed. Chill for 20 minutes.

With a mixer on high speed, beat egg whites until fluffy. Add sugar and beat until stiff peaks form. Place lemon filling in crust and top with peaked meringue. Brown in 400-degree oven for 5 to 6 minutes. Remove from oven and chill overnight in refrigerator. Yield: 8 servings.

FLOATING ISLAND

1 qt. milk
6 eggs (separated)
½ cup sugar
1 tbsp. vanilla
½ cup powdered sugar
2 tbsp. chocolate syrup

Put milk to boil. Beat egg yolks and sugar well. Stir the egg mixture into milk as it starts to boil. Stir constantly and cook for about 2 minutes until it begins to thicken. Add vanilla and remove from heat. Set in refrigerator to cool.

Beat the egg whites until stiff. Slowly add powdered sugar and continue to beat. Egg whites should be very stiff. The milk mixture should be cold. Pour milk mixture into a glass bowl. Spoon on stiffly beaten egg whites. Drizzle chocolate syrup very lightly over egg whites. Sprinkle with more powdered sugar. Serve very cold. The Creoles call this *La Neige* (the snow). Yield: 4 to 6 servings.

OLD-FASHIONED
BREAD PUDDING

1 loaf stale po' boy bread
   or 5 cups cubed stale
   white bread
2 12-oz. cans evaporated
   milk
1 cup water
6 eggs (beaten)
8 oz. crushed pineapple
1 large apple (grated)
1 cup raisins
1½ cups sugar
5 tbsp. vanilla
¼ lb. butter (softened)

In a bowl, break bread and moisten with evaporated milk and water. Pour eggs over mixture and mix well. Add pineapple, apple, raisins, sugar, and vanilla and mix well. Cut butter into pieces and add to mixture, mixing all ingredients well. Pour into a greased 9" x 13" baking dish. Bake at 350 degrees for 30 to 40 minutes. Can be served with ice cream or Bourbon Sauce (see index for recipe). Yield: 8 servings.

RICE CUSTARD

1 cup sugar
3 eggs (beaten)
1 tsp. vanilla
¼ tsp. cinnamon
¼ tsp. nutmeg
3 cups milk
2 cups cooked rice

Mix sugar with beaten eggs. Add vanilla, cinnamon, and nutmeg. Whip mixture well. Slowly add milk, mixing well. Add rice and mix well. Pour into a baking dish and sprinkle top with more nutmeg. Place baking dish in pan of hot water and put in 350-degree oven. Bake for 35 minutes or until custard is set. Yield: 4 servings.

FRUIT BOWL DELIGHT

1 6-oz. box instant vanilla
  pudding
3 cups whipping cream
1 32-oz. pkg. Oreo cookies
  (crumbled)
4 large bananas (sliced)
2 pt. fresh strawberries
  (cleaned and sliced)
4 large peaches (sliced)
1½ cups whipped cream

In a chilled mixing bowl, whip vanilla pudding powder and whipping cream together to make a thick custard. Chill for 30 minutes. In a serving bowl, place half of cookie crumbles, then layer half of the vanilla custard followed by half the bananas, half the strawberries, then half the peaches. Layer again with remaining custard, bananas, strawberries, and peaches. Top with whipped cream. May be garnished with whole fresh strawberries and sprigs of mint.

If fresh strawberries are not available, other fruits may be used or more fruits added. Other cookies may be substituted for Oreos. Yield: 6 to 8 servings.

STRAWBERRY CREPES

The only thing farmers in Madisonville grew lots of for money was strawberries. They would pick those and sell them to help their income. We were always like little ants, preparing for the winter in my father's garden. I used to tease my daddy and say it was my turn to be the grasshopper for awhile! Here is a good way to serve those delicious strawberries.

1 cup flour
½ tsp. salt
2 tbsp. butter
2 tbsp. sugar
½ cup milk
½ cup water
4 eggs
2 tbsp. brandy
1 tbsp. vanilla
Melted butter
Powdered sugar
2 pt. fresh strawberries
Whipped cream

Place flour, salt, butter, and sugar in mixer. Mix ingredients, slowly adding milk and water. Gradually add the eggs; mix well after each egg. Scrape bowl down, adding brandy and vanilla. Remove batter from mixer and let rest for 30 minutes. Brush 7-inch skillet with melted butter and heat. Pour 2 tablespoons batter in skillet and roll and tilt skillet to get a thin coating around bottom and sides. Brown the crêpe on one side and remove. Repeat with rest of batter. Set the crêpes on a warm platter and sprinkle with powdered sugar. Place a few strawberries (sliced) in the center of each crêpe and fold, end over end. Spoon a few strawberries on top and garnish with whipped cream. Yield: 6 to 8 crêpes.

CHOCOLATE CREPES
WITH STRAWBERRY FILLING

1 cup self-rising flour
1 tsp. sugar
2 eggs (beaten)
1 cup milk
2 tbsp. chocolate syrup
1 tbsp. chocolate liqueur
2 tbsp. melted butter
More melted butter for
    skillet

Sift flour; add sugar and mix in eggs. Add milk and mix well. Add chocolate syrup and liqueur. Beat mixture until smooth. Add the 2 tablespoons of melted butter and beat, making sure to remove all lumps. Brush 7-inch skillet with a little more melted butter. Heat skillet so that it is hot but won't burn. Pour in 2 tablespoons batter; tilt and roll skillet so that batter coats the bottom and sides. Brown on one side, then flip crêpe over. Cook for 2 minutes on other side. Remove and place on warm plate. Repeat for rest of batter. Place 1 tablespoon Strawberry Filling in each. Yield: 6 crêpes.

STRAWBERRY FILLING
1 tsp. cornstarch
1 cup water
2 tbsp. sugar
1 pt. strawberries (sliced)
1 tsp. Cointreau
1 tsp. strawberry liqueur

Mix cornstarch with water until all lumps are dissolved. Cook over medium heat until mixture thickens and turns clear. Add sugar and strawberries. Continue to cook on a slow heat. Add liqueurs. Cook until strawberries are just soft, about 5 minutes.

GINGERBREAD

¼ lb. butter (softened)
1 cup sugar
1½ cups syrup
3 cups flour
2 tsp. ground ginger
2 tsp. cinnamon
1 cup hot water
2 tsp. baking soda
3 eggs (beaten)

Preheat oven at 350 degrees. Grease a 9" x 13" baking pan.

In a large bowl, mix butter and sugar until well combined. Add the syrup and mix well. Gradually add flour, ginger, and cinnamon, mixing well after each addition. In a separate bowl pour the hot water over the soda and stir briefly.

Pour the soda mixture into the flour mixture and mix well. Add the beaten eggs and mix well. Pour into the greased baking pan and bake at 350 degrees for 45 minutes or until cake tests done by springing back up when pressed in the center. Yield: 16 squares.

FRUIT TARTS

8 oz. cream cheese
2 cups self-rising flour
1 cup butter
3 oz. instant vanilla pudding
2 cups whipping cream
Fresh fruit
Coconut flakes
Chopped nuts

Preheat oven at 300 degrees. In large bowl mix cream cheese, flour, and butter. Mix well until a dough forms. Set aside and let rest for 30 minutes. In a chilled mixing bowl, whip vanilla pudding powder and whipping cream together until a thick custard is formed. Place in refrigerator and chill.

Take dough and pinch off a ball about quarter-size for small tarts or dollar-size for large tarts. With slightly floured fingers, work dough into muffin tins until it contours to the pan. Bake at 300 degrees for 30 minutes or until shells become light brown. Remove from oven, then from pan, and cool on a rack. When cool, fill shells with custard, arrange fresh fruit on top, and garnish with coconut flakes and chopped nuts. Yield: 24 small tarts.

PECAN TARTS

8 oz. cream cheese
2 cups self-rising flour
1 cup butter
1 lb. brown sugar
1 egg
1 tsp. vanilla
1 cup chopped pecans
1 tbsp. butter

Preheat oven at 300 degrees. In a large mixing bowl combine cream cheese, flour, and the cup of butter. Mix well until a dough forms. Set aside and let rest for 30 minutes. In a bowl mix brown sugar, egg, vanilla, pecans, and the tablespoon of butter. Mix until sugar begins to dissolve.

Take dough and pinch off a ball about quarter-size for small tarts or dollar-size for large tarts. With slightly floured fingers, press the dough into muffin tins until the dough takes the shape of the tins. Place a teaspoon of the filling in the smaller tarts or a tablespoon of filling into the larger tarts. Bake for 30 to 35 minutes. Yield: 24 small tarts.

SUGAR PECANS

1 egg white
1 tsp. cold water
½ cup sugar
½ tsp. cinnamon
1 tsp. salt
1 lb. pecan halves

Beat egg white and water together in a bowl. Mix sugar, cinnamon, and salt in another bowl. Coat pecans in egg mixture, then stir coated pecans in sugar/spice mixture. Spread pecans in buttered shallow pan. Bake at 200 degrees for 1 hour. Shake pecans every 15 minutes. Yield: 2 cups.

PECAN DROPS

2 large egg whites
¾ cup light brown sugar
  (packed firmly)
½ tsp. vanilla
2 cups pecan halves

Beat egg whites to soft peaks. Beat in brown sugar and vanilla. Do not overbeat. Fold in pecans. Drop by teaspoon on greased aluminum foil on cookie sheet. Cook in oven for 30 minutes at 250 degrees. Turn oven off. Let drops remain in oven for another 30 minutes. Yield: 12 drops.

DEPRESSION CAKE

Using stale bread with Depression Cake works pretty well. If you let the cake get good and cold, it is just like eating pudding. What is nice is you don't have to do anything but let that bread soak up those juices and it will come out perfect.

4 pt. strawberries
2 cups sugar
12 oz. day-old po' boy
  bread or 6 slices stale
  white bread
1 lb. butter
8 oz. cream cheese
4 oz. strawberry liqueur
1 pt. whipping cream
  (whipped)
Whole strawberries for
  garnish

Clean strawberries, place in container with 1 cup of the sugar, and let sit overnight. Next day, butter a 10-inch springform cake pan, making sure to cover the entire ring and the bottom pan well. With a little extra sugar, sprinkle pan well and shake off excess.

Trim all crust off bread and slice bread in half. Mix butter and cream cheese in bowl. Coat all sides of bread with butter mixture and line half of it all around cake pan and bottom ring. Pour half of the sugared strawberries on top of bread with the liquid. Sprinkle berries with remaining cup of sugar. Layer another layer of bread with butter mixture down. Cover cake with plastic wrap. Place cake pan on baking pan and weight top of cake down with heavy pot. Place cake in refrigerator overnight.

Whip whipping cream until stiff. Blend remaining strawberries with strawberry liqueur. Unmold cake and place on serving dish. Frost cake with whipped cream and drizzle with the strawberry mixture. Garnish with whole strawberries.

BUTTER CAKE

Holidays were big things in the country. Those were the times we would get foods and gifts we didn't get any other time of the year. We didn't have any money at all and my mother would make stuffed animals out of scraps or whatever she had.

When we came home from the midnight mass on Christmas, we had stewed chicken. We didn't have turkey. If you didn't raise it, you didn't have it. We also had pork roast and duck. We just cooked everything we had. The idea was to cook plenty because it was Christmas. Mother's pride and joy was if she could get somebody to come from New Orleans and bring her a big fish. If she couldn't get a redfish or red snapper, her next choice was a gaspergou. She would boil it and use it as her centerpiece.

Always, in the country, we took great pains to make cakes for the holidays. We made cakes for two days straight before Christmas. The big thing in Madisonville was to be able to say you had six or seven cakes. Everybody, in all their Christmas clothes, went to everybody else's house to visit before the midnight mass (with someone always staying behind to receive the visitors). If I did not see you the whole year, I saw you on Christmas. The big thing was to see how many people would visit you at your house. All they did was say "Merry Christmas," you poured them some wine, gave them a piece of cake, and they went on to the next house.

There were jelly cakes mostly, or butter cakes, fruitcakes, cakes with chocolate or jelly toppings, and plain pound cakes. There weren't a lot of fancy cakes. You had to make sure you had enough for everybody who came around. This simple butter cake is the kind of thing we would have for those holidays.

> **1 lb. butter**
> **1 lb. confectioners' sugar**
> **6 eggs**
> **2⅔ cups cake flour (sifted)**
> **2 tsp. vanilla**

Preheat oven at 350 degrees. Grease a cake pan.

With a mixer set on high speed, cream butter and sugar until light and fluffy. Add eggs one at a time, mixing well after each egg. Gradually add flour, mixing well and scraping down sides of mixing bowl. After all flour has been added, add vanilla and mix for 1 minute. Pour into greased cake pan and bake for 1 hour or until a toothpick inserted into cake comes out clean.

SISTER'S FUDGE

This is my sister Cleo's fudge. She can make the best fudge in the world. It really is good fudge, but she has to have a certain pot to make it. You can't make this fudge in any old pot according to her. It has to be that particular pot or it is not going to come out right.

> **2 13-oz. cans evaporated**
> **milk**
> **3 cups sugar**
> **¼ lb. butter**
> **1 qt. chopped pecans**
> **4 tbsp. vanilla**

One thing to remember about making this fudge is timing. This recipe can only be perfected with precise and undisturbed timing.

In a 5-quart saucepot, mix evaporated milk and sugar and stir well. Place the saucepot on medium heat. Timing begins at this point. Stir for 30 minutes, making sure to stir around the sides as well as the middle of the pot. After the 30 minutes of stirring, add the butter and stir for 5 minutes. Add pecans and stir for 5 minutes. Add vanilla and stir for 5 minutes. Candy should appear to pull away from the sides of the pot.

Pour into a well-greased 9" x 13" pan. Let cool for 10 to 15 minutes and then cut into desired squares. Make sure to cut candy while still warm to prevent breakage.

Chocolate chips or cocoa can be added to enhance the chocolate flavor.

HOLIDAY COOKIES

**1 lb. red candied cherries
(chopped)**
**1 lb. green candied cherries
(chopped)**
**1 lb. candied pineapple
(chopped)**
1 lb. pecans (chopped)
15 oz. golden raisins
3 cups all-purpose flour
1 tsp. baking soda
1 tsp. cinnamon
1 tsp. nutmeg
1 tsp. ground cloves
**½ cup butter or margarine
(softened)**
**½ cup brown sugar
(packed firmly)**
4 eggs
½ cup bourbon
3 tbsp. milk

In a large bowl combine cherries, pineapple, pecans, raisins, and ½ cup of the flour. Toss mixture well to coat fruits and nuts. Set aside. In a small bowl mix remaining flour, soda, cinnamon, nutmeg, and cloves. Set aside. Using a rotary mixer cream butter. Gradually add brown sugar, beating until fluffy. Add eggs one at a time and beat well after every addition. Add flour mixture, bourbon, and milk. Mix well. Pour egg mixture over fruit and mix well.

Drop dough by teaspoonful onto a lightly greased cookie sheet. Bake at 300 degrees for 20 minutes. Remove from oven and cool. Yield: 9 dozen.

Index